RO...

LEARN TO PRAY

66 Bible Prayer Passages
Explained and Applied

BARBOUR

PUBLISHING

Our mission is to inspire the world with the life-changing message of the Bible.

Member of the
Evangelical Christian
Publishers Association

CONTENTS

INTRODUCTION

The ability to communicate is one thing that sets human beings apart from other living things. God made people in His own image, giving them emotions and creativity, as well as the language by which to share these things.

Very young children must learn to talk with other people, in a process that develops over time. Talking with God—or *prayer*—is also a skill that requires effort.

So how do we learn to pray?

To answer that question, we go to the Word of God—the Bible. It provides countless examples of and instructions about prayer that help us understand just what it is, how it's done, and why it's so essential to our lives.

Of course, the Bible is a large book, written thousands of years ago. Its size and antiquity can be daunting to us, causing us to miss the life-changing truths it shares. That's why we've created *Learn to Pray*.

In this little volume, you'll find brief entries on 66 aspects of prayer. Each entry summarizes a particular point, giving you a clearer view of one facet of communication with God. Every entry follows this outline:

- IN TEN WORDS OR LESS: A "nutshell" glance at the topic.
- DETAILS, PLEASE: A longer explanation, incorporating information from throughout God's Word.
- ADDITIONAL SCRIPTURES: A few other key verses supporting the point.
- WHAT OTHERS SAY: A memorable quotation from a pastor, theologian, or Christian author.
- SO WHAT? An inspirational or devotional thought as a personal takeaway.

Prayer is something you need to know and enjoy—direct communication with the God of the universe, the loving God who created you, keeps you, and offers you eternal life through His Son, Jesus Christ. Use this book to begin a journey of discovery that could truly change your life!

LEARN TO PRAY. . .with Regularity

IN TEN WORDS OR LESS
Various types of praying should be a normal Christian discipline.

DETAILS, PLEASE
The first biblical reference to prayer appears near the beginning of recorded history "Then began men to call on the name of the LORD" (Genesis 4:26). This spiritual communication with God is called *prayer*. People are to pray on God's terms at any time, in any place, about anything.

When Jesus' disciples heard Him pray, they realized that they had more to learn about prayer. To be able to pray like Him, they said, "Lord, teach us to pray" (Luke 11:1). This is an important part of Christian discipleship. When Saul of Tarsus became a Christian, one of the first things said about him was, "Behold, he is praying" (Acts 9:11 NKJV). Regular prayer is to be a joyful experience (John 16:23–24).

ADDITIONAL SCRIPTURES
- Praying always with all prayer and supplication in the Spirit, and watching thereunto with all perseverance and supplication for all saints. (Ephesians 6:18)
- Do not be anxious about anything, but in every situation, by prayer and petition, with thanksgiving, present your requests to God. (Philippians 4:6 NIV)
- Pray without ceasing. (1 Thessalonians 5:17)
- I exhort therefore that, first of all, supplications, prayers, intercessions, and giving of thanks, be made for all men. (1 Timothy 2:1)

WHAT OTHERS SAY
Prayer is God's appointed means for appropriating the blessings that are ours in Christ Jesus. *D. A. Carson*

SO WHAT?
To know the Lord and grow as a Christian, prayer must become a regular part of life It's like the joy that young children have when talking to their loving father.

LEARN TO PRAY. . .
Accepting God's Invitations

IN TEN WORDS OR LESS
God in heaven graciously invites people to talk with Him.

DETAILS, PLEASE
To those who request our company, accepting an invitation is a common courtesy. What's amazing is that God—who created all things and controls the universe—has reached out to us and *invites* us to pray to Him. That God wants us to spend time with Him, experiencing His presence, is incredible. And it is in our best interest to accept His invitation. Consider how God invited the prophet Jeremiah to pray when his faith was severely tested in difficult times: "Call unto me, and I will answer thee, and show thee great and mighty things, which thou knowest not" (Jeremiah 33:3).

ADDITIONAL SCRIPTURES
- Hear, O LORD, when I cry with my voice: have mercy also upon me, and answer me. When thou saidst, Seek ye my face; my heart said unto thee, Thy face, LORD, will I seek. (Psalm 27:7–8)
- And call upon me in the day of trouble: I will deliver thee, and thou shalt glorify me. (Psalm 50:15)
- Come now, and let us reason together, saith the LORD: though your sins be as scarlet, they shall be as white as snow; though they be red like crimson, they shall be as wool. (Isaiah 1:18)
- Come unto me, all ye that labour and are heavy laden, and I will give you rest. (Matthew 11:28)
- Draw near to God, and He will draw near to you. (James 4:8 ESV)

WHAT OTHERS SAY
While God is always ready to answer the cry of the human heart, man must first request assistance. *R. K. Harrison*

SO WHAT?
There is no greater invitation than one from God.

LEARN TO PRAY. . .
Expecting God's Answers

IN TEN WORDS OR LESS
Trust God to keep His promises to answer your prayers.

DETAILS, PLEASE
King Solomon said, "the LORD is far from the wicked, but He hears the prayer of the righteous" (Proverbs 15:29 NKJV). God told Israel that if they would assist others who cried for help, He would then answer them when they called to Him: "You shall call, and the LORD will answer; You shall cry, and He will say, 'Here I am'" (Isaiah 58:9 NKJV). If we live as God calls us to live, we can expect Him to respond to our prayers.

ADDITIONAL SCRIPTURES
- Again I say unto you, That if two of you shall agree on earth as touching any thing that they shall ask, it shall be done for them of my Father which is in heaven. (Matthew 18:19)
- Therefore I will look unto the LORD; I will wait for the God of my salvation: my God will hear me. (Micah 7:7)
- If ye abide in me, and my words abide in you, ye shall ask what ye will, and it shall be done unto you. (John 15:7)
- And this is the confidence that we have in him, that, if we ask any thing according to his will, he heareth us: and if we know that he hear us, whatsoever we ask, we know that we have the petitions that we desired of him. (1 John 5:14–15)

WHAT OTHERS SAY
The story of every great Christian achievement is the history of answered prayer. *E. M. Bounds*

SO WHAT?
A promise is only as good as the person who makes it. We can trust God always to give His best answers to our prayers.

LEARN TO PRAY. . .
Requesting God's Answer

IN TEN WORDS OR LESS
Believers can plead with God to answer their prayers.

DETAILS, PLEASE
"I beseech thee, O LORD God of heaven. . .let thine ear now be attentive, and thine eyes open, that thou mayest hear the prayer of thy
servant, which I pray before thee now" (Nehemiah 1:5–6). Calling
to the prayer-answering God, Nehemiah appealed to the fact that
he and others of God's servants were praying "day and night" (verse
6). He repeated his request in verse 11 (NKJV): "O Lord, I pray, please
let Your ear be attentive to the prayer of your servant." In Psalm 4:1
(NKJV) David also asked to be heard: "Hear me when I call, O God
of my righteousness!" He had confidence that when he prayed, God
was listening: "The LORD will hear when I call unto him" (verse 3).

ADDITIONAL SCRIPTURES
- Hearken therefore unto the supplications of thy servant. . .
  hear thou from thy dwelling place, even from heaven; and
  when thou hearest, forgive. (2 Chronicles 6:21)
- Give ear to my words, O LORD, consider my meditation.
  Hearken unto the voice of my cry, my King, and my God:
  for unto thee will I pray. (Psalm 5:1–2)
- Hear my prayer, O LORD, give ear to my supplications:
  in thy faithfulness answer me, and in thy righteousness.
  (Psalm 143:1)

WHAT OTHERS SAY
If your vision is so big that only God can accomplish it, then you
obviously must pray. *David Guzik*

SO WHAT?
We can ask God to do what He has promised to do—which is to
answer our prayers.

LEARN TO PRAY. . .
Expecting Various Answers

IN TEN WORDS OR LESS
God in His wisdom gives different answers to our prayers.

DETAILS, PLEASE
We human beings sometimes pray for things that are contrary to God's will, so He must give different answers to accomplish His good and wise plans for our lives. But we can always be sure that whatever God's answer is, it will be the best one. In scripture, God answers prayers four ways:

He says *yes* to some requests. Jabez believed that "the God of Israel" answered prayer and was the source of blessings. Jabez stood apart as a good man who was "more honorable" than his peers, and he prayed specifically for the growth and expansion of his influence, for God's presence to empower and guide him, and for protection from evil. Jabez believed in prayer and "God granted him that which he requested" (1 Chronicles 4:9–10).

God also answers *no* to certain requests. When Elijah was depressed, he prayed that God would end his life (1 Kings 19:4)—but that request was gently denied. God alone has authority over our appointed days, and He knew that denying Elijah's request was the best answer. In 2 Samuel 11–12 we see David attempting to hide his sexual sin with Bathsheba. God's prophet Nathan announced that because of this sin the couple's newborn child would die. David pleaded with God for the life of the boy, but the baby perished (verses 14–19). And the entire nation of Israel learned that God will not hear prayers because of widespread sin (Isaiah 1:15).

Sometimes God answers *wait* to requests. David learned about God's waiting room and advised others to "rest in the LORD, and wait patiently for him" (Psalm 37:7). He testified "I waited patiently for the LORD, and he inclined unto me, and heard my cry" (Psalm 40:1). David learned that God cannot be rushed, so sometimes patience is needed in dealing with Him.

Finally, sometimes God gives an unexpected answer to our requests. This is what the apostle Paul experienced when he repeatedly requested that his "thorn in the flesh" be removed (2 Corinthians

12:7–9). Though leaving a painful thorn in place didn't seem like a good option, Paul learned about God's sustaining grace from this experience—and it made him spiritually stronger.

ADDITIONAL SCRIPTURES
- Delight thyself also in the LORD: and he shall give thee the desires of thine heart. (Psalm 37:4)
- If I regard iniquity in my heart, the Lord will not hear me. (Psalm 66:18)
- O LORD, how long shall I cry, and thou wilt not hear! even cry out unto thee of violence, and thou wilt not save! (Habakkuk 1:2)
- O my Father, if it be possible, let this cup pass from me: nevertheless not as I will, but as thou wilt. (Matthew 26:39)

WHAT OTHERS SAY
No answer to prayer is an indication of our merit; every answer to prayer is an indication of God's mercy. *John Blanchard*

SO WHAT?
We should never be disappointed with how God's answers our prayers since He gives His best answer at the right time.

LEARN TO PRAY. . .
According to God's Power

IN TEN WORDS OR LESS
God's power is displayed in His ability to answer prayers.

DETAILS, PLEASE
In James 5:13–18, prayer is mentioned seven times. This reveals its importance and power. Prayer is beneficial for both our bodies and our souls, and it is a powerful means used by God to accomplish His will. James reminds us of Elijah's example in 1 Kings 17–18, describing him as a man just like us, one who offered prayers that even affected the weather. Then James makes this great declaration: "The prayer of a righteous person is very powerful in its effect" (James 5:16 CSB).

ADDITIONAL SCRIPTURES
- Now unto him that is able to do exceeding abundantly above all that we ask or think, according to the power that worketh in us, unto him be glory. (Ephesians 3:20–21)
- Ah Lord GOD! behold, thou hast made the heaven and the earth by thy great power and stretched out arm, and there is nothing too hard for thee. (Jeremiah 32:17)
- For the eyes of the LORD run to and fro throughout the whole earth, to shew himself strong in the behalf of them whose heart is perfect toward him. (2 Chronicles 16:9)
- For with God nothing shall be impossible. (Luke 1:37)

WHAT OTHERS SAY
There are many things outside the power of ordinary Christian people, but the humblest and least significant Christian can pray, and as "prayer moves the Hand that moves the world," perhaps the greatest power that we can exert is that which comes through prayer. *W. H. Griffith Thomas*

SO WHAT?
What we desire but cannot achieve on our own, God is able to do for us by His power. . .when we devote ourselves to prayer.

LEARN TO PRAY. . .Persistently

IN TEN WORDS OR LESS
Christians should constantly communicate with their heavenly Father.

DETAILS, PLEASE
Praying should be every Christian's daily activity. Regular praying is described as praying "day and night" (Psalm 88:1–2). Old Testament saints customarily prayed three times per day, as we see in another psalm: "Evening, and morning, and at noon, will I pray, and cry aloud: and he shall hear my voice" (55:17). The great prophet Daniel followed this same pattern (Daniel 6:10). Some people reason that if we *eat* three times a day for our bodies, *praying* daily at three appointed times would equally benefit our souls. The apostle Paul, who compared the Christian life to a kind of combat, recommended "praying always with all prayer and supplication in the Spirit, and watching thereunto with all perseverance and supplication for all saints" (Ephesians 6:18).

ADDITIONAL SCRIPTURES
- Pray without ceasing. (1 Thessalonians 5:17)
- God is my witness, whom I serve with my spirit in the gospel of his Son, that without ceasing I make mention of you always in my prayers. (Romans 1:9)
- Then He spoke a parable to them, that men always ought to pray and not to lose heart. (Luke 18:1 NKJV)
- Continue steadfastly in prayer, being watchful in it with thanksgiving. (Colossians 4:2 ESV)
- But we will give ourselves continually to prayer, and to the ministry of the word. (Acts 6:4)

WHAT OTHERS SAY
It is essential to your soul's health to make praying a part of the business of every twenty-four hours in your life. *J. C. Ryle*

SO WHAT?
If we don't pray regularly, we certainly won't get answers from God. In fact, we should recognize prayerlessness as sin, confessing it and asking God to make us people who are devoted to prayer.

LEARN TO PRAY. . .with Faith

IN TEN WORDS OR LESS
Our prayers must be characterized by our trust in God.

DETAILS, PLEASE
Hebrews 11 is filled with examples of what true faith looks like. Verses 5–6 describe the faith of Enoch, a man found in the book of Genesis, who was known for pleasing God. The Lord so enjoyed Enoch that he was taken to heaven without dying! When Jesus described His own relationship to His Father, He said, "I do always those things that please him" (John 8:29). God-pleasers are people who, according to Hebrews 11:6, "diligently seek him" through regular prayer and worship.

This faith that pleases God first accepts that God exists—and exists as He has revealed Himself in scripture. The Bible begins with a statement of God's existence: "In the beginning God. . ." (Genesis 1:1). And God has not left us to imagine what He is like since He describes Himself by His attributes, actions, and many names. But He's revealed best in the Person of His Son, Jesus Christ, through the "incarnation" (God taking on a human body). It pleases God when we trust His description of Himself, showing faith in a Person who is there!

This faith also believes that God rewards those who strive to know and honor Him. The prospect of God's reward encouraged Moses to live a life of devotion despite many hardships. Hebrews 11:26 (NKJV) says "he looked to the reward" which he viewed as "greater riches than the treasures of Egypt." God told His people that "ye shall seek me, and find me, when ye shall search for me with all your heart" (Jeremiah 29:13). And when people find God, they discover that He becomes to them their "exceeding great reward" (Genesis 15:1).

ADDITIONAL SCRIPTURES
- If any of you lacks wisdom, you should ask God, who gives generously to all without finding fault, and it will be given to you. But when you ask, you must believe and not doubt, because the one who doubts is like a wave of the sea, blown and tossed by the wind. (James 1:5–6 NIV)

- Jesus answered and said unto them, Verily I say unto you, If ye have faith, and doubt not, ye shall not only do this which is done to the fig tree, but also if ye shall say unto this mountain, Be thou removed, and be thou cast into the sea; it shall be done. And all things, whatsoever ye shall ask in prayer, believing, ye shall receive. (Matthew 21:21–22)
- Let us then approach God's throne of grace with confidence, so that we may receive mercy and find grace to help us in our time of need. (Hebrews 4:16 NIV)
- Trust in him at all times, you people; pour out your hearts to him, for God is our refuge. (Psalm 62:8 NIV)

WHAT OTHERS SAY

The greater the difficulty to be overcome, the more it will be seen to the glory of God how much can be done by prayer and faith. *George Müller*

SO WHAT?

Since our faith pleases God, we must trust in His faithfulness, power, and wisdom to do what He has promised.

LEARN TO PRAY. . .Fervently

IN TEN WORDS OR LESS
Fervent prayers are thoughtful, passionate, heartfelt, and serious.

DETAILS, PLEASE
Epaphras, a leader in the Colossian church, was commended for his personal prayer ministry. While away from his congregation, he faithfully prayed for them. As the apostle Paul described it Epaphras was "always labouring fervently" for his people in prayer (Colossians 4:12). This aligned with the prayer life God had described to Jeremiah centuries earlier—that if the people would seek God with all of their heart and pray, they would find God. Their prayers would be heard (Jeremiah 29:12–13).

ADDITIONAL SCRIPTURES
- I cried with my whole heart; hear me, O LORD: I will keep thy statutes. (Psalm 119:145)
- LORD, thou hast heard the desire of the humble: thou wilt prepare their heart, thou wilt cause thine ear to hear. (Psalm 10:17)
- The eyes of the LORD are upon the righteous, and his ears are open unto their cry. (Psalm 34:15)
- The LORD is nigh unto all them that call upon him, to all that call upon him in truth. He will fulfil the desire of them that fear him: he also will hear their cry and will save them. (Psalm 145:18–19)
- The LORD is far from the wicked: but he heareth the prayer of the righteous. (Proverbs 15:29)

WHAT OTHERS SAY
True prayer is neither a mere mental exercise, nor a vocal performance, but it is far deeper than that—it is spiritual commerce [transaction] with the Creator of heaven and earth. *Charles H. Spurgeon*

SO WHAT?
Learning to pray fervently will maximize your spiritual growth.

LEARN TO PRAY. . .with Thanksgiving

In Ten Words or Less
Prayer must include gratitude to God for His many blessings.

Details, Please
The attitude of gratitude is a repeated theme in Paul's letter to the Colossians, especially in chapter 3. First, in verse 15, Paul exhorts believers to be thankful for being part of a body of believers who live with each other in peace. In verse 16, he said that wherever the written word of Christ is richly honored, grateful praise will be produced. This theme of thanksgiving ends in verse 17 with an exhortation that all our words and actions should be in the name of Jesus, with thanksgiving. Gratitude blossoms as believers live in peace with each other and offer praise to God.

Additional Scriptures
- But thanks be to God which giveth us the victory through our Lord Jesus Christ. (1 Corinthians 15:57)
- Do not be anxious about anything, but in every situation, by prayer and petition, with thanksgiving, present your requests to God. (Philippians 4:6 NIV)
- In every thing give thanks: for this is the will of God in Christ Jesus concerning you. (1 Thessalonians 5:18)
- By him therefore let us offer the sacrifice of praise to God continually, that is, the fruit of our lips giving thanks to his name. (Hebrews 13:15)
- Let us come before his presence with thanksgiving, and make a joyful noise unto him with psalms. (Psalm 95:2)

What Others Say
God doesn't want us to just feel gratitude, but for us to show it by giving thanks to God with our lives. *R. C. Sproul*

So What?
We should constantly give thanks to God because our cup of blessing is always overflowing.

LEARN TO PRAY. . .Authentically

IN TEN WORDS OR LESS
Jesus taught that not all prayers are acceptable to God.

DETAILS, PLEASE
In Matthew 6, Jesus described two bad motives that make prayers unacceptable. First, He said, don't pray like a hypocrite who only wants to be seen by others (verse 5). To deal with this error, Jesus encouraged people to pray secretly, promising that God would then answer their prayers publicly (verse 6). Our interest should be people seeing our prayers answered rather than just watching us pray. The second error involved frivolous repetition to lengthen prayers, like religious pagans trying to manipulate their reluctant false gods (verse 7). Jesus explained that long prayers are unnecessary since the heavenly Father already knows His children's needs before they ask (verse 8). God enjoys hearing His children's voices and answering their requests.

ADDITIONAL SCRIPTURES
- If I regard iniquity in my heart, the Lord will not hear me. (Psalm 66:18)
- He that turneth away his ear from hearing the law, even his prayer shall be abomination. (Proverbs 28:9)
- Then they will cry out to the LORD, but he will not answer them. At that time he will hide his face from them, because of the evil they have done. (Micah 3:4 NIV)
- This people draweth nigh unto me with their mouth, and honoureth me with their lips; but their heart is far from me. (Matthew 15:8)

WHAT OTHERS SAY
We pray unto God for the purpose of honoring Him, acknowledging Him to be the Knower of our hearts and the Giver of all mercies. *Arthur W. Pink*

SO WHAT?
We may need to make adjustments in our prayer life to ensure there is nothing that would hinder God from answering us.

LEARN TO PRAY. . .Intimately

IN TEN WORDS OR LESS
When praying we can address God as our heavenly Father.

DETAILS, PLEASE
In Matthew 6:9, where Jesus gives instructions on how to pray, He taught that our prayers should begin with God—who should be addressed as "our heavenly Father." This title describes His transcendent nature, as God is distinct from what He has made. But the title also indicates His nearness to us. God's lofty position doesn't mean that He is hard to reach—it simply indicates that we should have reverence toward Him.

In one sense, God is the Father of everyone by virtue of creation (Psalm 100:3). But He is the spiritual Father only of individual believers, since He saves those who *believe* in Him: "For ye are all children of God by faith in Christ Jesus" (Galatians 3:26).

The tender title "Abba, Father" is found three times in the New Testament. It was used by the Lord Jesus (Mark 14:36) and the apostle Paul when addressing God in prayer (Galatians 4:6; Romans 8:15–16). The Aramaic word *Abba* is equivalent to the English title "Daddy" or "Papa" and was originally spoken by small children. When used in prayer, it indicates the intimacy found in a close family relationship between God and His believing children. It is by God's Spirit that people are lovingly adopted into God's family and motivated to address Him with this affectionate title.

Jesus' use of the plural pronoun *our* when addressing God as Father shows that we should remember others who are part of the worldwide family of believers.

ADDITIONAL SCRIPTURES
- Every good gift and every perfect gift is from above, and cometh down from the Father of lights, with whom is no variableness, neither shadow of turning. (James 1:17)
- For this cause I bow my knees unto the Father of our Lord Jesus Christ. (Ephesians 3:14)
- Now unto God and our Father be glory forever and ever. Amen. (Philippians 4:20)
- Jesus saith unto him, I am the way, the truth, and the life:

no man cometh unto the Father, but by me. (John 14:6)
- But the hour cometh, and now is, when true worshippers shall worship the Father in spirit and in truth: for the Father seeketh such to worship him. (John 4:23)

WHAT OTHERS SAY

If you want to judge how well a person understands Christianity, find out how much he makes of the thought of being God's child, and having God as his Father. If this is not the thought that prompts and controls his worship and prayers and his whole outlook on life, it means that he does not understand Christianity very well at all.
J. I. Packer

SO WHAT?

God gave us a memorable picture of His nature by comparing Himself to a good father: "As a father has compassion on his children, so the LORD has compassion on those who fear him" (Psalm 103:13 NIV).

LEARN TO PRAY. . .with Adoration

In Ten Words or Less
As our creator and redeemer, God deserves our constant praise.

Details, Please
When Jesus' disciples asked Him to teach them how to pray, He instructed them with what we call "the Lord's Prayer." This model prayer begins with adoration: "Our Father which art in heaven, Hallowed be thy name" (Luke 11:2). This idea—first focusing on God with praise and adoration—sets a pattern for many biblical prayers (see 1 Kings 8:22–24; Isaiah 37:15–16; Acts 4:24).

The book of Psalms, Israel's hymnbook of praise, is filled with adoration of God. Psalm 100 is totally dedicated to praise. In fact, the New International Version's title for this song reads, "A psalm. For giving grateful praise." The psalm begins by encouraging shouts of joy to the Lord. And it ends with a powerful reason for praise: "For the LORD is good" (verse 5). His mercy ("love," NIV) will never end.

Additional Scriptures
- O Lord, thou art my God; I will exalt thee, I will praise thy name; for thou hast done wonderful things; thy counsels of old are faithfulness and truth. (Isaiah 25:1)
- Thou art worthy, O Lord, to receive glory and honour and power: for thou hast created all things, and for thy pleasure they are and were created. (Revelation 4:11)
- Worthy is the Lamb that was slain to receive power, and riches, and wisdom, and strength, and honour, and glory, and blessing. (Revelation 5:12)

What Others Say
Praising and adoring God is the noblest part of the saint's work on earth, as it will be his chief employ in heaven. *Arthur W. Pink*

So What?
Adoration focuses on God's perfections. The more we learn about Him, the greater our praise becomes until the day that our praise is perfect in heaven.

LEARN TO PRAY. . .for God's Kingdom

IN TEN WORDS OR LESS
We should ask God for the arrival of His kingdom.

DETAILS, PLEASE
God's kingdom has different aspects. In the Old Testament book of Daniel, King Nebuchadnezzar—who viewed himself as earth's supreme authority—discovered that God rules sovereignly over all. Nebuchadnezzar learned that God's kingdom is everlasting (4:3), "the most High ruleth in the kingdom of men" (4:17), God sets up rulers (4:25), and accomplishes His sovereign plan in heaven and earth so that resistance is futile (4:35).

Christians, meanwhile, wait for God's kingdom to come to earth, which will bring heaven's blessings in a dramatic way (Luke 2:25, 38; Acts 1:6). When Jesus and John the Baptist preached, they announced that God's kingdom was "at hand" (or "near," Matthew 3:1–2; 4:17). Many of Jesus' followers hoped that God's promised kingdom would result in Israel's liberation from Roman oppression. But when the Roman governor Pilate examined Jesus to determine if He was a threat to the empire, Jesus clarified that His kingdom was a spiritual reality, and not of this world (John 18:36).

Jesus had told the Pharisees that His kingdom does not come "with observation," meaning there would not be dramatic outward changes (Luke 17:20–21). And the apostle Paul spoke of God's kingdom in its spiritual-mystery form. When sinners believe on Christ, God the Father rescues them from Satan's domain—"the power of darkness"—and transfers them into the kingdom of His beloved Son. Believers receive redemption by Jesus' blood and the forgiveness of sins (Colossians 1:12–14). Then, by the transforming power of God's Spirit, the kingdom grows in a believer's life. Moral qualities are developed, as Paul noted: "For the kingdom of God is not a matter of eating and drinking, but of righteousness, peace, and joy in the Holy Spirit" (Romans 14:17 NIV).

Believers continually look forward to the final stage of God's kingdom when "the kingdoms of this world are become the kingdoms of our Lord, and of his Christ; and he shall reign for ever and ever" (Revelation 11:15). Christians long to see the Lord Jesus exalted as King of kings and Lord of lords (Revelation 19:16). Until then we pray, "Even so come Lord Jesus" (Revelation 22:20) and, "Thy kingdom come, Thy will be done in earth, as it is in heaven" (Matthew 6:10).

ADDITIONAL SCRIPTURES

- But seek ye first the kingdom of God, and his righteousness; and all these things shall be added unto you. (Matthew 6:33)
- Fear not, little flock: for it is your Father's good pleasure to give you the kingdom. (Luke 12:32)
- Jesus answered and said unto him, Verily, verily, I say unto thee, Except a man be born again, he cannot see the kingdom of God. (John 3:3)
- The time is fulfilled, and the kingdom of God is at hand: repent ye, and believe the gospel. (Mark 1:15)

WHAT OTHERS SAY

Although Christ does not yet rule on earth, He is no less a king. In response to Pilate's question, "Are You the King of the Jews?" Jesus replied, "It is as you say" (Matthew 27:11). He reigns in eternity, rules now over His church, and one day will return to rule the earth as King of kings. *John MacArthur Jr.*

SO WHAT?

Christians are to help others enter God's kingdom, then wait and pray for the return of our glorious King.

LEARN TO PRAY. . .at Mealtime

IN TEN WORDS OR LESS
Times of eating are a good reminder to pray.

DETAILS, PLEASE
It's been suggested that every time we open our mouth to eat, we should also open our mouth to pray. Jesus taught that our nourishment is a subject that should be a matter of prayer (Luke 11:1–3). This encourages a short daily prayer for daily needs.

"Our daily bread" represents the ongoing provision of food by which God cares for our bodies. This subject may not seem spiritual—but when food is scarce, it finds its way to the top of prayer lists. Though for many of us today, it seems the request should be for God's help to keep us from eating too much!

Mealtime prayers highlight the issue of trust in God as our ultimate provider. We acknowledge that all that we have, even our daily food, comes from Him. He is known as Jehovah-Jireh, the God who provides (Genesis 22:14). And we should be grateful for what He gives (Acts 27:35).

In prayer, we can acknowledge the different ways that God provides. Sometimes it's through our own work. At other times, people generously share. On rare occasions God even provides through miracles—Israel was taught an important lesson about trusting God for daily needs as they ate His manna for forty years (Deuteronomy 8:3).

Finally, Jesus' wording "give *us*" helps us to remember others. We should strive to be charitable so the hungry around us can be blessed. All Christians are instructed to "do good to all men, especially them who are of the household of faith" (Galatians 6:10).

ADDITIONAL SCRIPTURES
- For we brought nothing into this world, and it is certain we can carry nothing out. And having food and raiment let us be therewith content. (1 Timothy 6:7–8)
- Whether therefore ye eat, or drink, or whatsoever ye do, do all to the glory of God. (1 Corinthians 10:31)

- "I have not departed from the commands of his lips; I have treasured the words of his mouth more than my daily bread." (Job 23:12 NIV)
- Every day they continued to meet together in the temple courts. They broke bread in their homes and ate together with glad and sincere hearts. (Acts 2:46 NIV)
- Keep falsehood and lies far from me; give me neither poverty nor riches, but give me only my daily bread. Otherwise, I may have too much and disown you and say, "Who is the LORD?" Or I may become poor and steal, and so dishonor the name of my God. (Proverbs 30:8–9 NIV)

WHAT OTHERS SAY

If we learn how to pray this petition biblically, it will help us in several areas. It will help us understand godly dependence, it will help us understand humility, it will help us understand gratitude and generosity and contentment, and even it will help us in making sure that our desires are placed on the right thing, are focused in the right place, that we desire the Giver more than we desire any gift that He gives. *J. Ligon Duncan*

SO WHAT?

Just as Jesus instructed us not to *worry* about necessary food, He also taught us to *depend* on God and pray that He would provide for our needs.

LEARN TO PRAY. . .
with Confession

We should seek forgiveness from God for our sins.

DETAILS, PLEASE

Jesus taught that we should regularly confess our sins in our prayers. As part of "the Lord's prayer," He taught this request: "And forgive us our debts, as we forgive our debtors" (Matthew 6:12). God is very forgiving, so He encourages us to confess our sins to Him. As David once prayed, "For thou, Lord, art good, and ready to forgive; and plenteous in mercy unto all them that call upon thee" (Psalm 86:5).

Our confessions of sin should be as frequent as our experience of guilt. God will reveal to us the transgressions He finds in our lives. David's prayer of self-examination is appropriate for us to repeat: "Search me O God, and know my heart: try me, and know my thoughts: and see if there be any wicked way in me, and lead me in the way everlasting" (Psalm 139:23–24).

Jesus wanted us to view our sins as a serious debt owed to God. We have broken His laws! And this sin-debt is beyond our ability to repay. Only Jesus' sacrificial death on the cross could make propitiation (that is, satisfy God) for our sins (Ephesians 1:7; 1 John 2:1–2).

As we confess our sins, Jesus taught us to include a prerequisite: asking God to forgive us in the same way that we forgive those who sin against us. We must always be forgiving people since God has forgiven us. It's not that we earn forgiveness from God when we forgive others, but we show that we have been forgiven—and we in turn forgive others as God has us (Matthew 18:21–35).

To "confess our sins" (1 John 1:9) literally means "to say the same thing" that God does. That's more than just admitting to sins—confession involves an honest and humble agreement about them. The confession of the prodigal son is a great example: "Father, I have sinned against heaven, and before thee, and am no more worthy to be called thy son: make me as one of thy hired servants" (Luke 15:18–19). God's promise of forgiveness in the second part of 1 John 1:9 gives us assurance of His faithful pardon and purification.

ADDITIONAL SCRIPTURES

- We have sinned, and committed iniquity, and done wickedly, and have rebelled, even by departing from thy precepts and from thy judgments. (Daniel 9:5)
- Let the wicked forsake his way, and the unrighteous man his thoughts: and let him return unto the LORD, and he will have mercy upon him; and to our God, for he will abundantly pardon. (Isaiah 55:7)
- I acknowledge my sin unto thee, and mine iniquity have I not hid. I said, I will confess my transgressions unto the LORD; and thou forgavest the iniquity of my sin. Selah. (Psalm 32:5)
- He that covereth his sins shall not prosper: but whoso confesseth and forsaketh them shall have mercy. (Proverbs 28:13)

WHAT OTHERS SAY

Forgiveness is always free. But that doesn't mean that confession is always easy. Sometimes it is hard. Incredibly hard. It is painful (sometimes literally) to admit our sins and entrust ourselves to God's care. *Erwin W. Lutzer*

SO WHAT?

Because God is holy, He wants us to examine our own lives to deal with our own sins. He welcomes our prayers for cleansing through confession.

LEARN TO PRAY. . .
with Forgiveness

In Ten Words or Less
Christians who have been forgiven must become forgiving

Details, Please
The subject of forgiveness follows closely after "the Lord's prayer" in Matthew 6. When people start following Jesus, they should also follow what He called the second greatest commandment—loving other people as yourself (Matthew 22:39). In Matthew 6:14–15, the specific issue is showing love by *forgiving* other people.

In Jesus' view, there is an inseparable connection between the forgiveness we receive from our heavenly Father and the forgiveness we extend to others. For Christians, withholding forgiveness is an act of disobedience. Because God has freely forgiven our unpayable debt against Him, we are to forgive whatever sins others commit against us—which by comparison are much smaller. This is the point of Jesus' parable of the unforgiving servant in Matthew 18:23–35.

To be absolutely clear, this is not teaching salvation by works, which would contradict the gospel of grace (Ephesians 2:8–9; Titus 3:5–7). What Jesus described was the power of the gospel to change us into forgiving people.

God's forgiveness has two aspects. The first is the *judicial* forgiveness that God as judge provides. This is a once-for-all pardon (justification) when a person joins God's family (John 5:24). The second is the *parental* forgiveness that God as our Father provides. This is the daily pardoning (sanctification) for a person who is part of God's family (John 13:8–10).

True forgiveness includes forgetting sins that have been committed against us. This is how God forgives us, as He said, "Their sins and iniquities I will remember no more" (Hebrews 10:17). Believers cannot allow a root of bitterness toward another person to remain in their lives. If you struggle with this, meditate on scriptures that describe importance of forgiveness in the Christian life, and keep praying until you are able to forgive fully. Nursing grudges can lead to God's faithful chastening (Hebrews 12:5–11).

ADDITIONAL SCRIPTURES

- Be ye kind to one another, tenderhearted, forgiving one another, even as God for Christ's sake hath forgiven you. (Ephesians 4:32)
- At my first answer no man stood with me, but all men forsook me: I pray God that it may not be laid to their charge. (2 Timothy 4:16)
- And if he trespass against thee seven times in a day, and seven times in a day turn again to thee, saying, I repent; thou shalt forgive him. And the apostles said unto the Lord, Increase our faith. (Luke 17:4–5)
- Forbearing one another, and forgiving one another, if any man have a quarrel against any: even as Christ forgave you, so also do ye. (Colossians 3:13)

WHAT OTHERS SAY

Hard hearts have no place in the kingdom of God. The reason, of course, is that the King himself is a forgiving king. Just as He forgives us when we rebel against Him, so the citizens of God's kingdom forgive one another. *R. Albert Mohler Jr.*

SO WHAT?

Forgiving others may be difficult—but the more we understand salvation, the clearer our duty becomes. It's also one of the best things we can do for ourselves.

LEARN TO PRAY. . .
for Spiritual Protection

IN TEN WORDS OR LESS
We can ask God to shield us from the devil.

DETAILS, PLEASE
In Matthew 6:13, Jesus teaches us to pray for each other, requesting God's help to safely navigate the spiritual minefield of this life. This prayer request is a safeguard when we are inevitably enticed to disobey God's Word. It recognizes our weakness toward sin and our inability to win battles in our own strength.

Jesus told us to pray, "Lead us not into temptation." We don't want to walk into situations in which we violate God's Word. And we can ask for continual deliverance from these tempting situations: "Deliver us from evil." God intends our trials to lead to positive results, accomplishing His good purposes and our spiritual growth (James 1:2–4). He wants to improve us while the devil tries to ruin us (1 Peter 5:8).

A growing hatred of evil can motivate us to pray this prayer regularly. We need more of the attitude of the psalmist, who said "Ye that love the LORD, hate evil" (Psalm 97:10). As our love for God increases, we become more sensitive to evil that He hates.

Scripture identifies our enemies so we can guard against them and win our spiritual battles. Ephesians 2:1–3 lists three: (1) "this world," a complex global system of people opposed to God (see also John 15:18–19); (2) the devil, called "the prince of the power of the air," who leads hordes of demons against us (see Matthew 9:34; by the way, his deceptions include denying his own existence to make people unaware of his presence); and (3) "the lusts of our flesh," our own corrupt human nature of selfish desires (see Mark 7:20).

When Peter denied Jesus, he learned—very painfully—the importance of prayer in confronting temptation (Matthew 26:40–41).

ADDITIONAL SCRIPTURES
- And the Lord said, Simon, Simon, behold, Satan hath desired to have you, that he may sift you as wheat: but I have prayed for thee, that thy faith fail not: and when thou art converted, strengthen thy brethren. (Luke 22:31–32)

- Put on the whole armour of God, that ye may be able to stand against the wiles of the devil. For we wrestle not against flesh and blood, but against principalities, against powers, against the rulers of the darkness of this world, against spiritual wickedness in high places. (Ephesians 6:11–12)
- I will lift up mine eyes unto the hills, from whence cometh my help. My help cometh from the LORD, which made heaven and earth. He will not suffer thy foot to be moved: he that keepeth thee will not slumber. (Psalm 121:1–3)
- But the Lord is faithful, and he will strengthen you and protect you from the evil one. (2 Thessalonians 3:3 NIV)
- "My prayer is not that you take them out of the world but that you protect them from the evil one." (John 17:15 NIV)

WHAT OTHERS SAY
We are taught to ask God to deliver us from the evil that is in the world, the evil that is within our own hearts, and not least from the evil one, the devil. *J. C. Ryle*

SO WHAT?
Christians should never underestimate spiritual enemies. Prayer for God's help is always needed as a safeguard.

LEARN TO PRAY. . .with Supplications

IN TEN WORDS OR LESS
Supplications are the specific requests that we ask of God.

DETAILS, PLEASE
One form of prayer called *supplications* (or "petitions," NASB) is mentioned twice in Ephesians 6:18. The term refers to urgent prayer requests for specific things we would like to have from God. When the apostle Paul writes of "supplication in the Spirit," he alludes to the Holy Spirit's influence on our requests so that we ask for scriptural things that align with God's will. And Paul notes that supplications are to be made "for all the saints" so that no one is omitted. God cares for everyone and wants us to have that same prayerful concern for each other.

ADDITIONAL SCRIPTURES
- Do not be anxious about anything, but in everything by prayer and supplication with thanksgiving let your requests be made known to God. (Philippians 4:6 ESV)
- These all continued with one accord in prayer and supplication, with the women, and Mary the mother of Jesus, and with his brethren. (Acts 1:14)
- I exhort therefore, that first of all, supplications, prayers, intercessions, and giving of thanks, be made for all men. (1 Timothy 2:1)
- Blessed be the LORD, because he hath heard the voice of my supplications. (Psalm 28:6)
- Then these men assembled, and found Daniel praying and making supplication before his God. (Daniel 6:11)

WHAT OTHERS SAY
You can do more than pray *after* you have prayed, but you cannot do more than pray *until* you have prayed. *John Bunyan*

SO WHAT?
Once Jesus asked two blind men, "What do you want me to do for you"? They requested their sight. Two questions for us: (1) What do we want? (2) Have we asked?

LEARN TO PRAY. . .for God's Will

IN TEN WORDS OR LESS
We should pray to do God's will despite our challenges.

DETAILS, PLEASE
On the night before Jesus' death He experienced prayerful sorrow and agony about doing God's will. He repeatedly prayed, "Father, if thou be willing, remove this cup from me: nevertheless, not my will, but thine, be done" (Luke 22:42). Jesus lived with a sense of accountability (John 5:30) and determination (John 4:34) regarding God's will. As Jesus completed His mission and cried out, "It is finished" (John 19:30), His prayers were shown to have been triumphant.

ADDITIONAL SCRIPTURES
- "Then I said, 'Here I am—it is written about me in the scroll—I have come to do your will, my God.'" (Hebrews 10:7 NIV)
- You need to persevere so that when you have done the will of God, you will receive what He has promised. (Hebrews 10:36 NIV)
- Forasmuch then as Christ hath suffered for us in the flesh, arm yourselves likewise with the same mind: for he that hath suffered in the flesh hath ceased from sin; that he should no longer live the rest of his time in the flesh to the lusts of men, but to the will of God. (1 Peter 4:1–2)
- And this is the confidence that we have in him, that, if we ask any thing according to his will, he heareth us. (1 John 5:14)

WHAT OTHERS SAY
Prayer is not a convenient device for imposing our will on God, or bending His will to ours, but the prescribed way of subordinating our will to His. *John R. W. Stott*

SO WHAT?
Our problems should not discourage us from praying but motivate us to persevere in prayer while we seek God's will.

LEARN TO PRAY. . .for Guidance

IN TEN WORDS OR LESS
We should request God's leading for all of life.

DETAILS, PLEASE
"Trust in the LORD with all thine heart; and lean not unto thine own understanding. In all thy ways acknowledge him, and he shall direct thy paths" (Proverbs 3:5–6). Notice that this divine promise of guidance is conditional. The verses instruct us to do three things:

First, "Trust in the LORD." Wholehearted trust in God involves taking the wisdom of His written word for guidance. Scripture records God's commands as well as moral and spiritual principals to follow to help us through this life. We should trust this divine revelation as our best guide for life. The psalmist understood this, writing, "Thy word is a lamp unto my feet, and a light unto my path" (Psalm 119:105).

Second, we are *not* to trust (or "lean on") our own understanding. Trusting in God's Word stands in direct contrast to what we would normally do—that is, base our beliefs on merely human wisdom and popular cultural ideas. Of course, these are frequently contrary to God's will. That's why Proverbs 28:26 says, "He that trusteth in his own heart is a fool." We must not rely on ideas that leave God out—and lead us astray.

Finally, we are to acknowledge God. Every decision that we make—indeed, every area of our lives—should be under His control. When these three conditions are met, God promises to guide us.

In those occasions when we are still uncertain about God's will, we can pray like King Jehoshaphat and all of Judah prayed when facing an impending enemy invasion. They prayed to God, "We do not know what to do, but our eyes are on you" (2 Chronicles 20:12 NIV)

ADDITIONAL SCRIPTURES
- "I am the LORD your God, who teaches you what is best for you, who directs you in the way you should go." (Isaiah 48:17 NIV)
- Shew me thy ways, O LORD; teach me thy paths. Lead me in thy truth and teach me: for thou art the God of my salvation; on thee do I wait all the day. (Psalm 25:4–5)

- Let the morning bring me word of your unfailing love, for I have put my trust in you. Show me the way I should go, for to you I entrust my life. . . . Teach me to do your will, for you are my God: may your good Spirit lead me on level ground. (Psalm 143:8, 10 NIV)
- Search me, O God, and know my heart: try me, and know my thoughts; and see if there be any wicked way in me, and lead me in the way everlasting. (Psalm 139:23–24)
- For thou art my rock and my fortress; therefore for thy name's sake lead me, and guide me. (Psalm 31:3)

WHAT OTHERS SAY

Wisdom is seeing life realistically from God's perspective. The Christian needing more wisdom, who repeatedly asks God to open his or her eyes and heart, can count on God repeatedly granting his or her request. *Thomas L. Constable*

SO WHAT?

When we need help with God's will during difficulties, guidance is available—in scripture and through prayer.

LEARN TO PRAY. . .with Fasting

IN TEN WORDS OR LESS
Foregoing food for a time may improve our praying.

DETAILS, PLEASE
Everyone agrees that prayer is important. But there is some uncertainty about *fasting*, since the New Testament contains examples rather than commands. The question of fasting arose in Jesus' day because His disciples didn't follow the practice (Matthew 9:14–15). Jesus explained that when the bridegroom is present, there should be feasting rather than fasting. That would change when Jesus left. Fasting would then be a matter of conscience.

ADDITIONAL SCRIPTURES
- And [Anna] was a widow of about fourscore and four years, which departed not from the temple, but served God with fastings and prayers night and day. (Luke 2:37)
- As they ministered to the Lord, and fasted, the Holy Ghost said, Separate me Barnabas and Saul for the work whereunto I have called them. And when they had fasted and prayed, and laid their hands on them, they sent them away. (Acts 13:2–3)
- And when they had ordained them elders in every church, and had prayed with fasting, they commended them to the Lord, on whom they believed. (Acts 14:23)
- Therefore also now, saith the LORD, turn ye even to me with all your heart, and with fasting, and with weeping, and with mourning. (Joel 2:12)

WHAT OTHERS SAY
Fasting. . .must not be confined to the question of food and drink; fasting should really be made to include abstinence from anything which is legitimate in and of itself for the sake of some special spiritual purpose. *D. Martyn Lloyd-Jones*

SO WHAT?
Scripture records many examples of people who fasted and prayed. We might find this voluntary activity helpful too.

LEARN TO PRAY. . .Privately

IN TEN WORDS OR LESS
Jesus taught His disciples the importance of praying alone.

DETAILS, PLEASE
Secret praying should be a priority. Jesus said, "Go into your room, close the door and pray to your Father who is unseen" (Matthew 6:6 NIV). God, who answers our prayers, is unseen—and we are not to pursue attention when we pray. Our secret praying will be rewarded, and any public praying we do should flow out of our private time with God. It's always better for God to see us praying in secret than for people to see us praying in public.

ADDITIONAL SCRIPTURES
- And when [Jesus] had sent the multitudes away, he went up into a mountain apart to pray: and when the evening was come, he was there alone. (Matthew 14:23)
- And in the morning, rising up a great while before day, [Jesus] went out, and departed into a solitary place, and there prayed. (Mark 1:35)
- But so much the more went there a fame abroad of him: and great multitudes came together to hear, and to be healed by him of their infirmities. And he withdrew himself into the wilderness, and prayed. (Luke 5:15–16)
- On the morrow, as they went on their journey, and drew nigh unto the city, Peter went up upon the housetop to pray about the sixth hour. (Acts 10:9)

WHAT OTHERS SAY
O, let the secret place of prayer become to me the most beloved spot on earth. *Andrew Murray*

SO WHAT?
Some are intimidated by praying before others, but God is pleased when He hears us pray before Him.

LEARN TO PRAY. . .Corporately

IN TEN WORDS OR LESS
Praying together is an important activity in Christian discipleship.

DETAILS, PLEASE
The storyline of Acts 12 encourages prayer meetings. As persecution of the early church intensified, believers met together to offer constant prayer (verses 5, 12). God answered their prayers by miraculously releasing Peter from the prison in which King Herod had held him (verses 7–11). Peter quickly made his way to the other believers, arriving at the house as their prayer meeting continued. You could say he knocked on their door while his friends were knocking on heaven's door! There was joyful surprise when Peter showed up and told his story (verses 13–17).

ADDITIONAL SCRIPTURES
- And when [Paul] had thus spoken, he kneeled down, and prayed with them all. (Acts 20:36)
- These all continued with one accord in prayer and supplication, with the women, and Mary the mother of Jesus, and with his brethren. (Acts 1:14)
- And when the time for the burning of incense came, all the assembled worshippers were praying outside. (Luke 1:10 NIV)
- Again I say unto you, That if two of you shall agree on earth as touching anything that they shall ask, it shall be done for them of my Father which is in heaven. (Matthew 18:19)

WHAT OTHERS SAY
We shall never see much change for the better in our churches in general until the prayer meeting occupies a higher place in the esteem of Christians. *Charles H. Spurgeon*

SO WHAT?
It's always good to commune with God through prayer, and the pattern of scripture includes believers meeting *together* to pray.

LEARN TO PRAY. . .during Illness

IN TEN WORDS OR LESS

We can raise our ailments to the God who heals.

DETAILS, PLEASE

"Is any among you afflicted?" the New Testament writer James asked. "Let him pray" (5:13). That's what the Old Testament king Hezekiah did. Isaiah 38 tells the story of his recovery from a serious illness through prayer and medical treatment.

Hezekiah had received a "thus saith the LORD" death sentence from the prophet Isaiah, who told the king, "Set thine house in order: for thou shalt die, and not live" (verse 1). With sorrow and a sense of self-preservation, Hezekiah called out for God to intervene (verses 2–3). He believed the prophet's warning, but he also believed that God hears and answers prayer. And God did, quickly sending Isaiah back to Hezekiah with a new message: he had been granted a reprieve of fifteen additional years of life (verses 4–5)! Hezekiah even received a miraculous sign as confirmation of this good news, when God reversed the sun's shadow for a time (verses 7–8). The king composed a song of thanksgiving to God for His intervention (verses 9–20).

The apostle Paul's story was different though. He prayed repeatedly that his "thorn in the flesh" might be removed, but it remained. God had something better for Paul, saying "my grace is sufficient" (2 Corinthians 12:7–9). "Sufficient grace" is a special power that God provides to believers to endure afflictions in a Christlike way. Their testimony shines during difficulties as they trust the Lord with thanksgiving and rejoicing.

Paul's thorn remained, so he adjusted his outlook, submitted to God's plan, and began praying for joyful endurance. He discovered that through his lingering weakness he depended more on Christ's power to sustain him. And Paul had new words of victory: "when I am weak, then am I strong" (verse 10).

ADDITIONAL SCRIPTURES

- Heal me, O LORD, and I shall be healed; save me, and I shall be saved: for thou art my praise. (Jeremiah 17:14)

- Bless the LORD, O my soul, and forget not all his benefits: who forgiveth all thine iniquities; who healeth all thy diseases. (Psalm 103:2–3)
- Then they cried to the LORD in their trouble, and he saved them from their distress. He sent out his word and healed them; he rescued them from the grave. (Psalm 107:19–20 NIV)
- Before I was afflicted I went astray: but now I have kept thy word. . . . It is good for me that I have been afflicted; that I might learn thy statutes. (Psalm 119:67, 71)
- And God shall wipe away all tears from their eyes; and there shall be no more death, neither sorrow, nor crying, neither shall there be any more pain: for the former things are passed away. (Revelation 21:4)

WHAT OTHERS SAY

If we must have a physician, let it be so, but still let us go to our God first of all; and, above all, remember that there can be no power to heal in medicine of itself; the healing energy must flow from the divine hand. *Charles H. Spurgeon*

SO WHAT?

God calls Himself Jehovah-Rapha, the LORD your healer. When He chooses to heal us, let's be sure to thank Him!

LEARN TO PRAY. . .for the Sick

IN TEN WORDS OR LESS
God can heal others through our prayers of faith.

DETAILS, PLEASE
James 5 speaks about church leaders who watch over our souls and visit the sick to offer prayer support. Verse 14 tells ailing people to "call for the elders of the church, and let them pray over him." The use of anointing oil may have medicinal or ceremonial significance. The prayer of faith should be offered, trusting in God's plan and power to heal (verse 15). Prayers confessing sins may also be needed (verse 16).

ADDITIONAL SCRIPTURES
- Beloved, I wish above all things that thou mayest prosper and be in health, even as thy soul prospereth. (3 John 2)
- And Moses cried unto the LORD, saying, Heal her now, O God, I beseech thee. (Numbers 12:13)
- But Hezekiah prayed for them, saying, The good LORD pardon everyone that prepareth his heart to seek God, the LORD God of his fathers, though he be not cleansed according to the purification of the sanctuary. And the LORD hearkened to Hezekiah, and healed the people. (2 Chronicles 30:18–20)
- [Publius's] father was sick in bed, suffering from fever and dysentery. Paul went in to see him and, after prayer, placed his hands on him and healed him. (Acts 28:8 NIV)

WHAT OTHERS SAY
God has made us members of Christ's body. If we do not share our needs and struggles with others, they cannot help bear our burdens and they will not rejoice when God answers. *Steven J. Cole*

SO WHAT?
Since sickness is common, we should pray according to God's will for mercy, grace, and healing.

LEARN TO PRAY. . .
for the Dying

In Ten Words or Less
Prayer can bring comfort to Christians facing death.

Details, Please
Psalm 23 describes a shepherd tending his sheep. The shepherd represents God caring for His people.

The writer of the psalm, David, began by discussing God in verses 1–3. Then he began to pray about encountering death: "Yea, though I walk through the valley of the shadow of death I will fear no evil: for thou art with me; thy rod and staff they comfort me" (verse 4).

David could be fearless and comforted on this dark walk because of the shepherd's presence. The tools in the shepherd's hands—the "rod" (a club) and the "staff" (a walking stick with a curved top)—both provided a sense of security from danger. The road in the valley was not a dead end, but one to "walk through"—to reach "the house of the Lord" where believers will live "forever" (verse 6). Centuries later, when the apostle Paul considered his many dangerous encounters, he said he was persuaded that not even death could separate believers from God's love in Christ Jesus our Lord (Romans 8:38–39).

The walk through this valley is inevitable—for everyone there is "a time to be born and a time to die" (Ecclesiastes 3:2). But to encourage those who have despair about death, David's son, Solomon, wrote, "the righteous hath hope in his death" (Proverbs 14:32). He knew that according to God's promise, believers will enjoy a glorious future in heaven forever.

During Jesus' crucifixion, the dying thief asked to be remembered after he died. Jesus gave the man this comforting promise: "Verily, I say unto thee, Today thou shalt be with me in paradise" (Luke 23:43). Paradise is described as a place where "God shall wipe away all tears from their eyes; and there shall be no more death, neither sorrow, nor crying, neither shall there be any more pain: for the former things are passed away" (Revelation 21:4).

- Precious in the sight of the LORD is the death of his saints. (Psalm 116:15)
- For to me, to live is Christ and to die is gain. . . . I am torn between the two: I desire to depart and be with Christ, which is better by far, but it is more necessary for you that I remain in the body. (Philippians 1:21, 23–24 NIV)
- And I heard a voice from heaven saying unto me, Write, Blessed are the dead which die in the Lord from henceforth: Yea, saith the Spirit, that they may rest from their labours; and their works do follow them. (Revelation 14:13)
- The LORD gave, and the LORD hath taken away; blessed be the name of the LORD. (Job 1:21)
- So teach us to number our days, that we may apply our hearts unto wisdom. (Psalm 90:12)

WHAT OTHERS SAY

Man is made capable of three births: by nature, he enters into the present world; by grace, into spiritual light and life; by death, into glory. *John Newton*

SO WHAT?

We can't change the fact that every one of us will eventually die. But through prayers of faith in God's promises we can face death with peace.

LEARN TO PRAY. . .with Intercessions

In Ten Words or Less
Praying for God's blessings on others is a high priority.

Details, Please
In 1 Timothy 2:1, the apostle Paul mentions different types of prayer including *intercession*—that is, praying for others. Prayer was to be "made for all people" (NIV). Even political authorities are included in these prayers, since they can help to create a peaceful society where the gospel can spread. This pleases "God our Savior" who wants everyone to be saved (verses 3–4). Prayer plays a major role in that pursuit.

Additional Scriptures
- Pray for us: for we trust we have a good conscience, in all things willing to live honestly. (Hebrews 13:18)
- Moreover as for me, God forbid that I should sin against the LORD in ceasing to pray for you: but I will teach you the good and the right way. (1 Samuel 12:23)
- Go to my servant Job, and offer up for yourselves a burnt offering; and my servant Job shall pray for you: for him will I accept: lest I deal with you after your folly, in that ye have not spoken of me the thing which is right, like my servant Job. (Job 42:8)
- Wherefore I also, after I heard of your faith in the Lord Jesus, and love unto all the saints, cease not to give thanks for you, making mention of you in my prayers. (Ephesians 1:15–16)

What Others Say
God has no greater controversy with His people today than this . . .there are so few who actually give themselves unto intercession. *Arthur Tappan Pierson*

So What?
It's normal for us to pray about our own needs, but we must also spend time praying for others.

LEARN TO PRAY. . .during Sorrow

In Ten Words or Less
God sees our tears and will hear our anguished prayers.

Details, Please
Hebrews 5:7 describes Jesus' praying as He anticipated dying on the cross. The "Man of Sorrows" felt grief in His soul and tears on His face—and He called to the One who could save Him. Jesus "was heard" because He prayed with great reverence. This example should encourage us because Jesus understands our sorrows. He's sympathetic to us (Hebrews 4:15), and "he is able to help those who are tempted" (Hebrews 2:18 CSB).

Additional Scriptures
- He is despised and rejected of men; a man of sorrows, and acquainted with grief: and we hid as it were our faces from him; he was despised, and we esteemed him not. (Isaiah 53:3)
- Thou tellest my wanderings: put thou my tears into thy bottle: are they not in thy book? (Psalm 56:8)
- Blessed are they that mourn: for they shall be comforted. (Matthew 5:4)
- For thou hast delivered my soul from death, mine eyes from tears, and my feet from falling. (Psalm 116:8)
- I will be glad and rejoice in your love, for you saw my affliction and knew the anguish of my soul. (Psalm 31:7 NIV)

What Others Say
Christ shed tears as well as blood for a lost world: He offered up strong cries and tears. By this He showed the truth of His humanity, and that He did not accept only the human nature, but did also assume human affections. *William Burkitt*

So What?
Jesus wept at Lazarus's grave, during the triumphal entry, and in Gethsemane. We are never alone in our sorrow—in all our affliction, Jesus is afflicted too.

LEARN TO PRAY. . .in Jesus' Name

IN TEN WORDS OR LESS
Acceptable prayers to God must be prayed in Jesus' name.

DETAILS, PLEASE
The night before Jesus' death He gave His disciples new instructions about prayer. He indicated that the prayers God would accept must be offered in Jesus' name (John 14:13–14). These answered prayers would produce lasting spiritual fruit (John 15:16), would honor God (John 15:7–8), and bring joy to the worshipper (John 16:23–24). Jesus gave the promises; now we must pray in His name.

ADDITIONAL SCRIPTURES
- Whatsoever ye do in word or deed, do all in the name of the Lord Jesus, giving thanks to God and the Father by him. (Colossians 3:17)
- "Salvation is found in no one else, for there is no other name under heaven given to mankind by which we must be saved." (Acts 4:12 NIV)
- I have manifested thy name unto the men which thou gavest me out of the world: thine they were, and thou gavest them me; and they have kept thy word. (John 17:6)
- Giving thanks always for all things unto God and the Father in the name of our Lord Jesus Christ. (Ephesians 5:20)

WHAT OTHERS SAY
To pray in Jesus' name means to pray with His authority, according to His will, with His approval, consistent with who He is. . . to pray exactly what Jesus would pray in any particular situation.
Ray Pritchard

SO WHAT?
We must understand that "praying in Jesus' name" is not a magical password to getting our prayers answered. It is an indication of our trust in all that Jesus taught about prayer.

LEARN TO PRAY. . .in the Spirit

IN TEN WORDS OR LESS
The Holy Spirit provides aid and influence in our prayers.

DETAILS, PLEASE
According to Ephesians 6:18, the Holy Spirit plays an influential role in our prayers. Believers should be "praying always with all prayer and supplication *in the Spirit*." This is not a special kind of prayer but praying in agreement with God's will as recorded in scripture, the sword of the Spirit (verse 17). Our prayers "in the Spirit" will align with the Spirit's morality (4:30–31) and the Spirit's fruit produced in us (5:9).

ADDITIONAL SCRIPTURES
- But you, dear friends, by building yourselves up in your most holy faith and praying in the Holy Spirit, keep yourselves in God's love as you wait for the mercy of our Lord Jesus Christ to bring you to eternal life. (Jude 20–21 NIV)
- And I will pour upon the house of David, and upon the inhabitants of Jerusalem, the spirit of grace and of supplications. (Zechariah 12:10)
- For ye have not received the spirit of bondage again to fear; but ye have received the Spirit of adoption, whereby we cry, Abba, Father. (Romans 8:15)
- Now I beseech you, brethren, for the Lord Jesus Christ's sake, and for the love of the Spirit, that ye strive together with me in your prayers to God for me. (Romans 15:30)

WHAT OTHERS SAY
When you pray in the Holy Spirit, the Spirit of God is "moving" you to pray. That is, He is the one who motivates and enables and energizes your prayer. And when you pray in the Holy Spirit, the Spirit of God is "guiding" how you pray and what you pray for. *John Piper*

SO WHAT?
Prayer is not something that we do alone. We're to pray to the Father, through the name of the Son, *by the power of the Spirit*.

LEARN TO PRAY. . .with Boldness

IN TEN WORDS OR LESS
We can approach God in prayer with confidence.

DETAILS, PLEASE
Because believers have a sympathetic great High Priest who represent them in heaven, we are encouraged to "come boldly unto [God's] throne of grace" (Hebrews 4:16). Other English Bible versions render the King James term *boldly* in phrases like "with confidence" (NIV). We can prayerfully approach God's throne with a settled assurance of His acceptance in our time of need. There we find *mercy* (addressing our past misery and failures) and find *grace* (for blessings that are sought when needed). In a sense, our exalted High Priest holds out His scepter for us to approach His throne, then asks, "How can I help you"?

ADDITIONAL SCRIPTURES
- Let us draw near with a true heart in full assurance of faith, having our hearts sprinkled from an evil conscience, and our bodies washed with pure water. (Hebrews 10:22)
- In him and through faith in him we may approach God with freedom and confidence. (Ephesians 3:12 NIV)
- For since he himself has suffered when he was tempted, he is able to help those who are tempted. (Hebrews 2:18 CSB)
- Wherefore he is able to save them to the uttermost that come unto God by him, seeing he ever liveth to make intercession for them. (Hebrews 7:25)

WHAT OTHERS SAY
All Christians, the youngest, the weakest, the most ignorant, have been made nigh and have constant freedom of access to God as believer-priests through their High Priest, Jesus Christ. *Jack L. Arnold*

SO WHAT?
It's encouraging to cast our cares on the One who cares for us. He provides exactly what we need and He waits to help us.

LEARN TO PRAY. . .for Sanctification

IN TEN WORDS OR LESS
Devotion to Christian living should be a matter of prayer.

DETAILS, PLEASE
1 Thessalonians 5:23–24 is a prayer-wish for God's lifelong sanctifying work—that is, His ongoing process of making believers more Christlike. To be sanctified means to be set apart *for* God and *from* evil. This progressive work of God continues until the individual's death or Jesus returns. Since the apostle's request in 1 Thessalonians 5 is for believers to be "wholly" sanctified, it means that every area of life must be consecrated—our actions, thoughts, and words—so we can be found blameless until the day the Lord returns. Paul ends by writing, "Brethren, pray for us" (verse 25).

ADDITIONAL SCRIPTURES
- It is God's will that you should be sanctified: that you should avoid sexual immorality. (1 Thessalonians 4:3 NIV)
- Sanctify them through thy truth: thy word is truth. . . . And for their sakes I sanctify myself, that they also might be sanctified through the truth. (John 17:17, 19)
- If anyone cleanses himself from these things, he will be a vessel for honor, sanctified, useful to the Master, prepared for every good work. (2 Timothy 2:21 NASB)
- Search me, O God, and know my heart: try me, and know my thoughts: and see if there be any wicked way in me, and lead me in the way everlasting. (Psalm 139:23–24)

WHAT OTHERS SAY
Though I am not what I ought to be, nor what I wish to be, nor what I hope to be, I can truly say, I am not what I once was. . .I can heartily join with the apostle, and acknowledge, "By the grace of God I am what I am." *John Newton*

SO WHAT?
God said, "Be holy, for I am holy" (Leviticus 11:45). We are to use the practical means of His Word, our fellowship together, and prayer to become more like Him.

LEARN TO PRAY. . .for Generosity

IN TEN WORDS OR LESS
God gives to us when we provide for others.

DETAILS, PLEASE
The book of Proverbs contains truths for wise living. It was written primarily by King Solomon, who received his wisdom from God—and was considered the wisest man on earth (1 Kings 4:29–30). According to Proverbs 21:13, "Whoso stoppeth his ears at the cry of the poor, he also shall cry himself, but shall not be heard." The sowing and reaping principle shows up here in the negative, but Proverbs 11:25 says, "A generous person will prosper; whoever refreshes others will be refreshed" (NIV). God loves cheerful givers and promises to bless them (2 Corinthians 9:6–8).

ADDITIONAL SCRIPTURES
- "In everything I did, I showed you that by this kind of hard work we must help the weak, remembering the words the Lord Jesus himself said: 'It is more blessed to give than to receive.'" (Acts 20:35 NIV)
- He that oppresseth the poor reproacheth his Maker: but he that honoureth him hath mercy on the poor. (Proverbs 14:31)
- Whoever is kind to the poor lends to the LORD, and he will reward them for what they have done. (Proverbs 19:17 NIV)
- And do not forget to do good and to share with others, for with such sacrifices God is pleased. (Hebrews 13:16 NIV)
- Command [the rich] to do good, to be rich in good deeds, and be generous and willing to share. (1 Timothy 6:18 NIV)

WHAT OTHERS SAY
Make no mistake: Every believer who helps the poor for the right reasons can count on God's blessing. *R. C. Sproul*

SO WHAT?
God owns everything. And He has entrusted us with more than we need so we can become like Him—willing to share with others as He leads.

LEARN TO PRAY. . .for Children

IN TEN WORDS OR LESS
God helps parents with their children by way of prayer.

DETAILS, PLEASE
In Matthew 19:13–15, Jesus tenderly shows the importance of children to God. He had previously invited everyone to come to Himself (11:28), but now He invited only little children. Parents brought their young ones to Jesus so He would touch them and pray for them. The parents were happy. The children were happy. The only ones *un*happy with Jesus' children's ministry, it seems, were the disciples. To them, this must have seemed like an interruption to the more important work—with adults. But Jesus was very clear: "Let the little children come to me, and do not hinder them" (19:14 NIV).

Certainly, prayer has an important place in family life. When the Bible gives instructions on Christian living in the home, instructions about prayer are not far behind. In Ephesians 6, the apostle Paul gave guidance to parents and children (verses 1–4) and soon described regular prayer (verse 18). He also followed this pattern in Colossians, with family instructions in 3:18–21 and a call to prayer in 4:2.

A story from church history highlights the power of a mother's prayers. Around the fifth century, a woman named Monica made it her mission to constantly pray for her son who needed to know the Lord. That young man, named Augustine, eventually became a renowned Christian leader who authored *The Confessions*. At one point, Monica told Augustine, "There was only one reason, and one reason alone why I wished to remain a little longer in this life, and it was to see you become a Christian." In later years Augustine could look back and recognize the importance of his mother's perseverance in prayer to his own salvation and ministry.

ADDITIONAL SCRIPTURES
- Lo, children are an heritage of the LORD; and the fruit of the womb is his reward. (Psalm 127:3)
- Arise, cry out in the night: in the beginning of the watches pour out thine heart like water before the face of the LORD: lift up thine hands toward him for the life of thy young children. (Lamentations 2:19)

- And it was so, when the days of their feasting were gone about, that Job sent and sanctified them, and rose up early in the morning, and offered burnt offerings according to the number of them all: for Job said, It may be that my sons have sinned, and cursed God in their hearts. Thus did Job continually. (Job 1:5)
- And all thy children shall be taught of the LORD; and great shall be the peace of thy children. (Isaiah 54:13)

WHAT OTHERS SAY

Let us plead very earnestly that God may by His Spirit enlighten our hearts to know this our calling—as parents to intercede and prevail for our children. *Andrew Murray*

SO WHAT?

Parenting is a very difficult job. But God is a very wise and loving Father who is happy to help.

LEARN TO PRAY. . .for Politicians

IN TEN WORDS OR LESS
Christians should pray for governmental leaders to further God's kingdom.

DETAILS, PLEASE
Praying for politicians is a priority in scripture. "I exhort, therefore, that, first of all, supplications, prayers, intercessions, and giving of thanks, be made for all men," the apostle Paul wrote, "for kings and for all that are in authority" (1 Timothy 2:1–2). Good citizenship should accompany these prayers to complement the gospel message (1 Peter 2:12–17). We can improve our government through our prayers.

ADDITIONAL SCRIPTURES
- And seek the peace of the city whither I have caused you to be carried away captives, and pray unto the LORD for it: for in the peace thereof shall ye have peace. (Jeremiah 29:7)
- Remind the people to be subject to rulers and authorities, to be obedient, to be ready to do whatever is good. (Titus 3:1 NIV)
- That which they have need of. . .let it be given to them day by day without fail: that they may offer sacrifices of sweet savours unto the God of heaven, and pray for the life of the king, and of his sons. (Ezra 6:9–10)
- If my people, which are called by my name, shall humble themselves, and pray, and seek my face, and turn from their wicked ways, then I will hear from heaven, and will forgive their sin, and heal their land. (2 Chronicles 7:14)

WHAT OTHERS SAY
Even when we cannot respect men or women in authority, we must respect their offices and pray for them. In fact, it is for our own good that we do so. *Warren W. Wiersbe*

SO WHAT?
When we are frustrated by the governance of our cities, states, and nation, God has given us a practical outlet for our energies: prayer.

LEARN TO PRAY. . .for Jerusalem

IN TEN WORDS OR LESS
We should pray for Jerusalem to find peace in Christ.

DETAILS, PLEASE
God calls us to "pray for the peace of Jerusalem" (Psalm 122:6). Known as "the city of peace," it has a long history of war and suffering. The answer to a prayer for Jerusalem's peace is found in Jesus Christ, who has made peace through the blood of His cross (Colossians 1:20). He has instituted a gospel of peace (Ephesians 6:15) so that people can have peace with God (Romans 5:1). Efforts for peace in Jerusalem keep failing, but according to Bible prophecy, lasting peace will be established when "the Prince of Peace" returns (Isaiah 9:6–7).

ADDITIONAL SCRIPTURES
- Ye that make mention of the LORD, keep not silence, and give him no rest, till he establisheth, and till he make Jerusalem a praise in the earth. (Isaiah 62:7)
- Do good in thy good pleasure unto Zion: build thou the walls of Jerusalem. (Psalm 51:18)
- How blessed is the man whose strength is in You; in whose heart are the highways to Zion! (Psalm 84:5 NASB)
- I say then, Hath God cast away his people? God forbid. For I [Paul] also am an Israelite, of the seed of Abraham, of the tribe of Benjamin. (Romans 11:1)
- Brethren, my heart's desire and prayer to God for Israel is, that they might be saved. (Romans 10:1)

WHAT OTHERS SAY
Those that can do nothing else for the peace of Jerusalem can pray for it, which is something more than showing their good-will; it is the appointed way of fetching in mercy. *Matthew Henry*

SO WHAT?
Christians have a kinship with the Jews since Jesus Himself was Jewish. We should pray for their wellbeing, and the wellbeing of their most important city.

LEARN TO PRAY. . .for Understanding

IN TEN WORDS OR LESS
Learning God's truth comes through prayer, study, and God's Spirit.

DETAILS, PLEASE
Paul's continual prayer for the Colossians was that they would grow in understanding of God's truth. In Colossians 1:9 the apostle prayed for them to "be filled with the knowledge of his will in all wisdom and spiritual understanding." This "increasing in the knowledge of God" is intended to produce a worthy walk and good works (verse 10). It takes God's power working in people to accomplish this (verse 11).

ADDITIONAL SCRIPTURES
- I pray that the eyes of your heart may be enlightened in order that you may know the hope to which he has called you. (Ephesians 1:18 NIV)
- Open my eyes, that I may see wondrous things from Your law. (Psalm 119:18 NKJV)
- Indeed, if you call out for insight and cry aloud for understanding. . .then you will understand the fear of the LORD and find the knowledge of God. (Proverbs 2:3, 5 NIV)
- What we have received is not the spirit of the world, but the Spirit who is from God, so that we may understand what God has freely given us. (1 Corinthians 2:12 NIV)

WHAT OTHERS SAY
[In Colossians 1:9–10] the sequence is important: first, wisdom; then walk; then work. I cannot work for God unless I am walking with Him; but I cannot walk with Him if I am ignorant of His will. The believer who spends time daily in the Word and prayer will know God's will and be able to walk with Him and work for Him.
Warren W. Wiersbe

SO WHAT?
Since learning God's truth is a lifelong process, we should continually seek His help to understand His truth.

LEARN TO PRAY. . .for Spiritual Strength

IN TEN WORDS OR LESS
God strengthens the souls of those who call on Him.

DETAILS, PLEASE
Since life's challenges can drain our inner strength, we can pray for needed power. In Ephesians 3:16, Paul asked that believers be "strengthened with might by his Spirit in the inner man" (see also Ephesians 1:19; 3:7). The "inner man" is humanity's spiritual part, and the apostle said that "though our outward man perish, yet the inward man is renewed day by day" (2 Corinthians 4:16). This spiritual strength is given from God's never-ending, glorious riches. Paul explained that his aim in prayer was "that Christ may dwell in your hearts by faith" (Ephesians 3:17). This "indwelling" refers to Christ feeling at home in our lives, providing power for deeper experiences between Himself and His people.

ADDITIONAL SCRIPTURES
- I can do all things through Christ which strengtheneth me. (Philippians 4:13)
- Finally, my brethren, be strong in the Lord, and in the power of his might. (Ephesians 6:10)
- Blessed are those whose strength is in you, whose hearts are set on pilgrimage. . . . They go from strength to strength, till each appears before God in Zion. (Psalm 84:5, 7 NIV)
- In the day when I cried thou answeredst me, and strengthenedst me with strength in my soul. (Psalm 138:3)
- He giveth power to the faint; and to them that have no might he increaseth strength. (Isaiah 40:29)

WHAT OTHERS SAY
A faithful God does not expect you to do what you cannot; He supplies the needed strength. *Erwin W. Lutzer*

SO WHAT?
Physical strength normally decreases with age. But our spirits can grow ever stronger through God's power.

LEARN TO PRAY. . .about Christ's Love

IN TEN WORDS OR LESS
Understanding the love of God requires a lifetime of prayer.

DETAILS, PLEASE
One of the great themes in the Bible is God's love. Many people begin learning about that from John 3:16. Another important passage, from the apostle Paul, is Ephesians 3:14–21. Specific emphasis on God's love is in verses 17–19. So, what can we learn?

Paul uses two metaphors in verse 17 to emphasize our need to be firmly established in God's love—"That Christ may dwell in your hearts by faith." First, there's an agricultural reference: Christians are to be "rooted" in love. The idea is of a strong tree being nourished by a good root system. Then we find an architectural reference, of a Christian's life being "grounded" in love. The idea is of a building constructed on a firm foundation.

Once we are established in Christ's love, we can go even farther. Paul said he wants people to "be able to comprehend" Christ's love (verse 18). This refers to a growing understanding of it, and the learning is done best "with all saints" rather than in isolation. As Psalm 66:16 says, "Come and hear, *all ye that fear God*, and I will declare what he has done for my soul" (emphasis added).

The apostle wants Christians to grasp the different dimensions of love—the "breadth, and length, and depth, and height" of it (verse 18). God's love is broad enough to reach all mankind (Ephesians 2:16), it's long enough to last for eternity (2:7), it's deep enough to reach condemned sinners (2:1), and high enough to exalt them to heaven (2:6).

In Ephesians 3:19, Paul prays that believers might "know" the love of Christ—that is, to experience what has been learned and see this love in action. This love of Christ "passeth knowledge," which indicates that there is always more to learn and experience.

What better cause for prayer?

ADDITIONAL SCRIPTURES
- A new commandment I give unto you, That ye love one another; as I have loved you, that ye also love one another. (John 13:34)

- Seeing ye have purified your souls in obeying the truth through the Spirit unto unfeigned love of the brethren, see that ye love one another with a pure heart fervently. (1 Peter 1:22)
- Greater love hath no man than this, that a man lay down his life for his friends. (John 15:13)
- Herein is love, not that we loved God, but that he loved us, and sent his Son to be the propitiation for our sins. (1 John 4:10)
- And walk in love, as Christ also hath loved us, and hath given himself for us an offering and a sacrifice to God for a sweetsmelling savour. (Ephesians 5:2)

WHAT OTHERS SAY

[In Ephesians 3] Paul is saying that he wants you to have the ability to grasp the love of Christ in your soul. He wants you as a believer to have a real, personal experience and comprehension of the incomparable love of Christ. *J. Ligon Duncan*

SO WHAT?

Everyone is welcome to enjoy God's love! Pray David's prayer from Psalm 69: "Hear me, O LORD; for thy loving kindness is good: turn unto me according to the multitude of thy tender mercies."

LEARN TO PRAY. . .for Salvation

IN TEN WORDS OR LESS
True faith will lead to a prayer for salvation.

DETAILS, PLEASE
God gives eternal life as a gift when it is requested. Romans 10:13 speaks of *praying* for salvation: "For whosoever shall call upon the name of the Lord shall be saved." Just a few verses earlier, God had promised that if anyone confesses Jesus as Lord and believes in His resurrection from His sacrificial death, that person would be saved (verse 9). The apostle Paul quotes the Old Testament prophet Joel in verse 13, saying, "For whosoever shall call upon the name of the Lord shall be saved" (see Joel 2:32). Salvation is gained through a prayer of faith.

ADDITIONAL SCRIPTURES
- The LORD is near to all who call on him, to all who call on him in truth. (Psalm 145:18 NIV)
- And when he was gone forth into the way, there came one running, and kneeled to him, and asked him, Good Master, what shall I do that I may inherit eternal life? (Mark 10:17)
- Then I called upon the name of the LORD; O LORD, I beseech thee, deliver my soul. (Psalm 116:4)
- God be merciful to me a sinner. (Luke 18:13)
- And he said unto Jesus, Lord, remember me when thou comest into thy kingdom. (Luke 23:42)

WHAT OTHERS SAY
It's not the prayer that saves; it's the repentance and faith behind the prayer that lay hold of salvation. *J. D. Greear*

SO WHAT?
If you feel the need for God's salvation, it's good to know that He accepts everyone who receives His Son.

LEARN TO PRAY. . .Evangelistically

IN TEN WORDS OR LESS
If we want to see people saved, we must pray.

DETAILS, PLEASE
In Romans 9–11 the apostle Paul focused attention on the nation of Israel, describing his emotional concern for them to be saved. Paul had "great heaviness and continual sorrow" (9:2) for those who would miss out on God's salvation and instead experience His judgment (6:23).

The error keeping Israel from salvation was self-righteousness—trusting their own works instead of Jesus' righteousness (10:2–4). The Israelites mistakenly thought that their religious heritage and practices made them acceptable to God. Unfortunately, they were religious but still lost.

Paul's burden for Israel—which we should all feel toward the unsaved—led to two important actions. One was his preaching, teaching, and testifying about the gospel of Christ (1:15–16; 10:14–15). The other was his *praying* for their conversion: "Brethren, my heart's desire and prayer to God for Israel is, that they might be saved" (10:1). If people are going to be saved, someone must ask God to do His saving work in their hearts. Paul determined to do everything necessary for other people to experience the salvation he had received (1 Corinthians 9:19–22).

The apostle's feelings reflected God's love for all sinners. In Ezekiel 33:11, the Lord said, "I have no pleasure in the death of the wicked; but that the wicked turn from his way and live." Jesus was also "moved with compassion" when He saw multitudes of people who were like sheep without a shepherd. This led Him to encourage prayer to the Lord of the harvest to send more laborers into His harvest (Matthew 9:36–38). Praying for people to be saved is a great expression of love.

In Romans 11:25–27, Paul prophesied about Israel's future, "all Israel shall be saved." One day, the apostle's desire for Israel will be realized—his prayer will be answered. On our own prayer lists, let's put names of people we want to see saved and joining us in heaven.

ADDITIONAL SCRIPTURES

- I exhort therefore, that, first of all, supplications, prayers, intercessions, and giving of thanks, be made for all men. . . for this is good and acceptable in the sight of God our Saviour; who will have all men to be saved, and to come unto the knowledge of the truth. (1 Timothy 2:1, 3–4)
- You who answer prayer, to you all people will come. (Psalm 65:2 NIV)
- The Lord is not slack concerning His promise, as some count slackness, but is longsuffering toward us, not willing that any should perish but that all should come to repentance. (2 Peter 3:9 NKJV)
- Continue earnestly in prayer, being vigilant in it with thanksgiving; meanwhile praying also for us, that God would open to us a door for the word, to speak the mystery of Christ, for which I am also in chains. (Colossians 4:2–3 NKJV)

WHAT OTHERS SAY

If we really desire the salvation of men, we shall pray for it. *Charles Hodge*

SO WHAT?

There may be no greater intercession than asking God to save a person's soul.

LEARN TO PRAY. . .for Revival

IN TEN WORDS OR LESS
Spiritual renewal is sent by God in answer to prayer.

DETAILS, PLEASE
Psalm 80 was Israel's prayer for national revival and restoration. The people asked God to "return" to them with His blessing (verse 14). They prayed, "revive us, and we will call on your name" (verse 18 NIV). A chorus appears repeatedly, "Restore us. . .make your face shine on us, that we may be saved" (verses 3, 7, 19 NIV). To intensify their request, the people expand God's name each time they call: First, "O God" (verse 3). Then "O God of hosts" (verse 7). Finally, "O Lord God of hosts" (verse 19). Revival is *God's* work, creating in people a humble turning from sin to obedience (2 Chronicles 7:14).

ADDITIONAL SCRIPTURES
- Wilt thou not revive us again: that thy people may rejoice in thee? (Psalm 85:6)
- Thus saith the high and lofty One that inhabiteth eternity, whose name is Holy; I dwell in the high and holy place, with him also that is of a contrite and humble spirit, to revive the spirit of the humble, and to revive that heart of the contrite ones. (Isaiah 57:15)
- A prayer of Habakkuk the prophet. . . O LORD I have heard thy speech and was afraid: O LORD, revive thy work in the midst of the years make known; in wrath remember mercy. (Habakkuk 3:1–2)
- You who have made me see many troubles and calamities will revive me again; from the depths of the earth you will bring me up again. (Psalm 71:20 ESV)

WHAT OTHERS SAY
No great spiritual awakening has begun anywhere in the world apart from united prayer—Christians persistently praying for revival. *J. Edwin Orr*

SO WHAT?
Prayers for revival should start with our own hearts, then move on to our churches, and finally to our nation.

LEARN TO PRAY. . .for Gospel Preaching

IN TEN WORDS OR LESS
Successful gospel preaching requires prayerful support from God's people.

DETAILS, PLEASE
In Ephesians 6, the apostle Paul described the power of satanic evil that opposes the progress of the gospel. Verses 18–20 identify intercessory prayer as the key to overcoming these dark forces. Paul recommended that all types of prayer should be used (verse 18). He expected God to help him proclaim the gospel, so he asked specifically for Christians to pray that God would empower him to deliver his messages in a worthy manner (verses 19–20). Paul wanted his messages to be both clear in their content and bold in their delivery. The Ephesian church could help him by interceding for him.

Paul first requested prayer that he could be clear about the "mystery of the gospel" (verse 19). He wanted God to make him a good apologist for the truth. To the church in Colosse, Paul asked for prayer that God would open doors of opportunity for him to speak (Colossians 4:3). He undoubtedly wanted God to open people's hearts and minds to understand and accept the truth, like He opened Lydia's heart when she was converted (Acts 16:14).

In Ephesians 6, Paul asked twice for prayer that he could speak "boldly" (verses 19–20). He did not want to be intimidated into silence or hold back anything that would further his mission. As he wrote, the apostle was in jail because of his preaching. Now he was asking for prayer to be courageous and faithful in this task.

It should be observed that while Paul was a prisoner "in chains" (verse 20 NIV), he did not ask prayer for his own comfort, safety, or release. Paul's primary concern was the furthering of God's kingdom, which would happen as people prayed.

ADDITIONAL SCRIPTURES
- And pray for us, too, that God may open a door for our message, so that we may proclaim the mystery of Christ, for which I am in chains. (Colossians 4:3 NIV)
- Pray for us that the message of the Lord may spread rapidly and be honored, just as it was with you. (2 Thessalonians 3:1 NIV)

- And now, Lord, behold their threatenings: and grant unto thy servants, that with all boldness they may speak thy word. (Acts 4:29)
- But I will stay on at Ephesus until Pentecost, because a great door for effective work has opened to me, and there are many who oppose me. (1 Corinthians 16:8–9 NIV)

WHAT OTHERS SAY

Even the apostle Paul wants to be prayed for with regard to his gospel ministry. . . . This is a reminder that Christians are to faithfully intercede for their ministers. *J. Ligon Duncan*

SO WHAT?

If we want to see the preaching of God's Word bear fruit, we must pray.

LEARN TO PRAY. . .for More Missionaries

IN TEN WORDS OR LESS
The church must ask God for more gospel workers.

DETAILS, PLEASE
As His crowd of followers increased, Jesus needed more helpers. His solution was prayer: "Ask the Lord of the harvest, therefore, to send out workers into his harvest field" (Matthew 9:38 NIV). This prayer was motivated by love, since Jesus knew every individual's needs in the large crowds following Him (verse 36). This request for gospel workers was the best solution possible, one that we can still be part of today.

ADDITIONAL SCRIPTURES
- Say not ye, There are yet four months, and then cometh harvest? behold, I say unto you, Lift up your eyes, and look on the fields; for they are white already to harvest. (John 4:35)
- Pray for us that message of the Lord may spread rapidly and be honored, just as it was with you. (2 Thessalonians 3:1 NIV)
- The fruit of the righteous is a tree of life; and he that winneth souls is wise. (Proverbs 11:30)
- Go ye therefore and teach all nations, baptizing them in the name of the Father, and the Son, and of the Holy Ghost. (Matthew 28:19)
- Also I heard the voice of the Lord, saying, Whom shall I send, and who will go for us? Then said I, Here am I; send me. (Isaiah 6:8)

WHAT OTHERS SAY
God has willed that His miraculous work of harvesting be preceded by prayer. It is God's way before He does a great work to pour a Spirit of supplication upon His people so that they plead for the work. *John Piper*

SO WHAT?
The Lord of the harvest works through prayer. As we are involved in the harvest ourselves, we can pray that others will join us.

LEARN TO PRAY. . .with Humility

IN TEN WORDS OR LESS
A proper view of self is essential for effective praying.

DETAILS, PLEASE
In 2 Chronicles 7, Solomon dedicated the new temple, the house of worship he'd built in Jerusalem. Then the Lord appeared with advice about the future—words of warning (verses 13–14), words of acceptance (verses 15–18), and words about judgment (verses 19–22). The Lord's warning explained how forgiveness and restoration could be gained if judgment came, and humble prayer was required: "If my people, which are called by my name, shall humble themselves, and pray, and seek my face, and turn from their wicked ways; then I will hear from heaven, and will forgive their sin, and will heal their land (verse 14).

ADDITIONAL SCRIPTURES
- Let nothing be done through strife or vainglory; but in lowliness of mind let each esteem other better than themselves. Look not every man on his own things, but every man also on the things of others. (Philippians 2:3–4)
- I tell you, this man went down to his house justified rather than the other: for every one that exalteth himself shall be abased; and he that humbleth himself shall be exalted. (Luke 18:14)
- Be clothed with humility: for God resisteth the proud, and giveth grace to the humble. (1 Peter 5:5)
- He hath shewed thee, O man, what is good; and what doth the LORD require of thee, but to do justly, and to love mercy, and to walk humbly with thy God? (Micah 6:8)

WHAT OTHERS SAY
Man is never sufficiently touched and affected by the awareness of his lowly state until he has compared himself with God's majesty. *John Calvin*

SO WHAT?
Self-reliant people try to control life's difficulties, but humble people share their concerns with the One who cares—and can help.

LEARN TO PRAY. . .for Unity

In Ten Words or Less
We should pray, like Jesus, for believers to be one.

Details, Please
Jesus prayed for the unity of believers, asking His Father "that they all may be one; as thou, Father, art in me, and I in thee, that they also may be one in us: that the world may believe that thou hast sent me" (John 17:21). Galatians 3:28 states that a spiritual unity exists among all true believers, making them "all one in Christ Jesus" despite racial, social, and gender distinctions. But this practical unity requires effort (Ephesians 4:1–3). Prayer is the starting point.

Additional Scriptures
- Now the God of patience and consolation grant you to be likeminded one toward another according to Christ Jesus: that ye may with one mind and one mouth glorify God, even the Father of our Lord Jesus Christ. (Romans 15:5–6)
- Endeavouring to keep the unity of the Spirit in the bond of peace. (Ephesians 4:3)
- Now I beseech you, brethren, by the name of our Lord Jesus Christ, that ye all speak the same thing, and that there be no divisions among you; but that ye be perfectly joined together in the same mind and in the same judgment. (1 Corinthians 1:10)
- Behold, how good and how pleasant it is for brethren to dwell together in unity! (Psalm 133:1)

What Others Say
Let us endeavour to keep the unity of the Spirit in the bond of peace, praying that all believers may be more and more united in one mind and one judgment. Thus shall we convince the world of the truth and excellence of our religion, and find more sweet communion with God and His saints. *Matthew Henry*

So What?
Prayer is the answer to the many issues that divide Christians today.

LEARN TO PRAY. . .with Watchfulness

In Ten Words or Less
In serious times, we must give serious attention to prayer.

Details, Please
The idea of watchfulness is being alert and ready for potential danger. Watchful people are keenly aware of what's happening around them. In the Old Testament, the sons of Issachar in David's army were like this. They "had understanding of the times, to know what Israel ought to do" (1 Chronicles 12:32). In our own struggles in the Christian life, this kind of commitment to prayer must be a priority. Through prayer, we can become "first responders" in any serious situation. Epaphras, who was well-known to the Colossian church, was a great example as he was "always laboring fervently" for this church in his prayers (Colossians 4:12).

Watchful prayer is repeatedly recorded in the book of Acts. "These all continued with one accord in prayer" (Acts 1:14). "And they continued steadfastly. . .in prayers" (2:42). "But we will give ourselves continually to prayer" (6:4). "Prayer was made without ceasing of the church unto God for [Peter]" (12:5).

Various circumstances require watchful praying. As the time of Jesus' death approached, He warned about the intense struggles that He and His disciples would encounter at Gethsemane and Golgotha, warning them to "watch and pray" (Matthew 26:41). Paul was concerned about false teaching and error spreading in the Colossian church, which he addressed throughout Colossians 2 before advising the people to "devote yourselves to prayer, being watchful" (Colossians 4:2 NIV). In his letter to the Ephesians, Paul spoke of Christian spiritual warfare and the use of prayer as a weapon (6:18). And the apostle Peter spoke of the importance of using our remaining time on earth wisely by being faithful to pray (1 Peter 4:7).

Watchful prayer, according to Paul, should also include thankfulness (Colossians 4:2). We must never forget to express gratitude for the work that God has done, what He is doing, and what He will do.

Additional Scriptures
- Watch and pray, that ye enter not into temptation: the spirit

indeed is willing, but the flesh is weak. (Matthew 26:41)

- Watch ye therefore, and pray always, that ye may be accounted worthy to escape all these things that shall come to pass. (Luke 21:36)
- The end of all things is at hand: be ye therefore sober, and watch unto prayer. (1 Peter 4:7)
- And pray in the Spirit on all occasions with all kinds of prayers and requests. With this in mind, be alert and always keep on praying for all the Lord's people. (Ephesians 6:18 NIV)

WHAT OTHERS SAY

Prayer is the most noble and necessary ministry that God entrusts to His children, but it is also the most neglected ministry. *D. Edmond Hiebert*

SO WHAT?

The world we live in is no friend of the Christian faith. When we "watch and pray," God will bless us with His presence and protection.

LEARN TO PRAY. . .for Comfort

In Ten Words or Less
Prayer calls down God's help for life's troubling situations.

Details, Please
Scripture praises God as the "the Father of mercies and the God of all comfort" (2 Corinthians 1:3). These titles indicate that He can provide what's needed when we are troubled. The next verse states that God "comforteth us in all our tribulation." The literal meaning of the word *comfort* is to come alongside someone to help.

This blessing is provided "that we may be able to comfort them which are in any trouble, by the comfort wherewith we ourselves are comforted of God." God doesn't comfort us to make us comfortable, but to make us comforters to other people.

Additional Scriptures
- Blessed are they that mourn: for they shall be comforted. (Matthew 5:4)
- I remembered thy judgments of old, O LORD; and have comforted myself. (Psalm 119:52)
- I, even I, am he that comforteth you: who art thou that thou shouldest be afraid of a man who shall die, and the son of man who shall be made as grass; and forgettest the LORD thy maker? (Isaiah 51:12–13)
- Now our Lord Jesus Christ himself, and God, even our Father. . .comfort your hearts, and stablish you in every good word and work. (2 Thessalonians 2:16–17)

What Others Say
Your Savior went without comfort so you might have it. He postponed joy so you might share in it. He willingly chose isolation so you might never be alone in your hurt and sorrow. *Joni Eareckson Tada*

So What?
Comfort is found in the sources that God provides: His Spirit (John 14:16–17), His Word (Psalm 119:52), and His people (1 Corinthians 1:4). Pray for His blessing through each.

LEARN TO PRAY. . .without Indifference

IN TEN WORDS OR LESS
Sometimes we don't pray because we don't recognize prayer's value.

DETAILS, PLEASE
In Isaiah's day, Israel saw that when sin increases, praying decreases. God gave His diagnosis of the nation: "But you have not called upon Me, O Jacob; and you have been weary of Me, O Israel" (Isaiah 43:22 NKJV). The people had abandoned prayer and God knew why—they had become weary of Him. Their prayerlessness was the fruit of sad indifference: "No one calls on your name or strives to lay hold of you" (Isaiah 64:7 NIV). The prophet Samuel believed that not praying was sinful: "As for me, God forbid that I should sin against the LORD in ceasing to pray for you" (1 Samuel 12:23).

ADDITIONAL SCRIPTURES
- Ye lust, and have not: ye kill, and desire to have, and cannot obtain: ye fight and war, yet ye have not, because ye ask not. (James 4:2)
- Have all the workers of iniquity no knowledge? who eat up my people as they eat bread, and call not upon the LORD. (Psalm 14:4)
- They are all hot, like an oven, and have devoured their judges; all their kings have fallen. None among them calls upon Me. (Hosea 7:7 NKJV)
- So the captain came to him, and said to him, "What do you mean, sleeper? Arise, call on your God; perhaps your God will consider us, so that we may not perish." (Jonah 1:6 NKJV)

WHAT OTHERS SAY
To be a Christian without prayer is no more possible than to be alive without breathing. *Martin Luther*

SO WHAT?
If prayer is not a normal part of our lives, we should confess this as sin to God—and start praying!

LEARN TO PRAY. . .without Selfishness

IN TEN WORDS OR LESS
Our prayers should include requests for God's blessing on others.

DETAILS, PLEASE
James 4:3 indicates that God doesn't answer all prayers, especially selfish ones: "When you ask, you do not receive, because you ask with wrong motives, that you may spend what you get on your pleasures" (NIV). In other words, prayers with unworthy motives will be rejected. To receive answers to our prayers, we must first meet God's conditions. Ask yourself, "*Why* am I praying what I'm praying"? When our own will is valued more than God's will, a prayer has a self-centered agenda. Before we pray, we should "find out what pleases the Lord" (Ephesians 5:10 NIV). Then we can pray to His glory.

ADDITIONAL SCRIPTURES
- Whether therefore ye eat, or drink, or whatsoever ye do, do all to the glory of God. (1 Corinthians 10:31)
- All a person's ways seem pure to them, but motives are weighed by the LORD. (Proverbs 16:2 NIV)
- For the LORD seeth not as man seeth; for man looketh on the outward appearance, but the LORD looketh on the heart. (1 Samuel 16:7)
- "I the LORD search the heart and examine the mind, to reward each person according to their conduct, according to what their deeds deserve." (Jeremiah 17:10 NIV)
- Let the words of my mouth, and the meditation of my heart, be acceptable in thy sight, O LORD, my strength, and my redeemer. (Psalm 19:14)

WHAT OTHERS SAY
Prayer is a mighty instrument, not for getting man's will done in heaven, but getting God's will done on earth. *Robert Law*

SO WHAT?
When praying, our desires should always be second to the Lord's desires. If we are uncertain, we can simply ask that His will be done.

LEARN TO PRAY. . .with Marital Unity

IN TEN WORDS OR LESS
Being considerate in marriage contributes to God answering our prayers.

DETAILS, PLEASE
The Bible says that marriage is good. It's a God-ordained institution of a man and a woman covenanting together to become one (Genesis 2:24). Jesus showed His approval of marriage by blessing a wedding in Cana of Galilee (John 2:1–11).

When two Christians unite in marriage, they should also unite in prayer. Peter, who was married (Matthew 8:14), spoke of this in 1 Peter 3:7: "Likewise, ye husbands, dwell with them according to knowledge, giving honor unto the wife, as unto the weaker vessel, and as being heirs together of the grace of life; that your prayers be not hindered."

Peter gave husbands two instructions: to give their wives understanding and give them honor. For husbands to "dwell with [their wives] according to knowledge" (verse 7), men must first learn their responsibility as loving leaders in the home, thinking biblically about their role. They should also learn their wives' needs, directly from the source! The bottom line is this: husbands can learn from scripture, from their wives, and from their mistakes.

Peter continued by saying that husbands are to give "honor unto the wife, as unto the weaker vessel." This recognizes that men and women are inherently different, with women normally being more delicate. Peter's teaching is intended to help husbands be more sensitive to their wives, since God expects that she should be respected. A good example is the husband of the Proverbs' "virtuous woman": he "praises" his wife (Proverbs 31:28 NIV). Women have an equal share in the blessings of eternal life as members of God's family, Peter noted. They are "heirs together of the grace of life."

Ultimately, a good marriage leads to an effective prayer life. Peter emphasized this again in verse 12, by saying "the eyes of the Lord are over the righteous, and his ears are open unto their prayers."

ADDITIONAL SCRIPTURES
- Marriage should be honored by all, and the marriage bed

kept pure, for God will judge the adulterer and the sexually immoral. (Hebrews 13:4 NIV)

- Whoso findeth a wife findeth a good thing, and obtaineth favour of the LORD. (Proverbs 18:22)
- Husbands, love your wives, even as Christ also loved the church, and gave himself for it. (Ephesians 5:25)
- Enjoy life with your wife, whom you love, all the days of this meaningless life that God has given you under the sun. (Ecclesiastes 9:9 NIV)
- " 'For this reason a man will leave his father and mother and be united to his wife, and the two will become one flesh.' So they are no longer two, but one flesh. Therefore what God has joined together, let no one separate." (Matthew 19:5–6 NIV)

WHAT OTHERS SAY

Indeed, to true believers, prayer is so invaluable that the danger of hindering it is used by Peter as a motive why, in their marriage relationships, and household concerns, they should behave themselves with great wisdom. *Charles H. Spurgeon*

SO WHAT?

If you're married and struggling to see answers to prayer, ask yourself how you're treating your spouse.

LEARN TO PRAY. . .Using the Psalms

IN TEN WORDS OR LESS
Praying the psalms will make our prayers more biblical.

DETAILS, PLEASE
Our prayers improve when we make the prayers of scripture our own prayers. For example, in Acts 4, Christians prayed two relevant psalms. In verse 24 they prayed, "Lord, thou art God, which hast made heaven, and earth, and the sea, and all that in them is." (This is from Psalm 146.) They continued in Acts 4:25 by praying, "Why did the heathen rage and the people imagine vain things?" (This is from Psalm 2.) Jonah found that praying from the psalms was helpful as he prayed from the belly of the great fish—every verse in his prayer recorded in Jonah 2 is from the psalms. The psalms lend themselves readily to the prayers of God's people.

ADDITIONAL SCRIPTURES
- I will extoll thee, my God, O king; and I will bless thy name for ever and ever. Every day will I bless thee; and I will praise thy name for ever and ever. (Psalm 145:1–2)
- Hear my prayer, O LORD, and let my cry come unto thee. Hide not thy face from me in the day when I am in trouble; incline thine ear unto me: in the day when I call answer me speedily. (Psalm 102:1–2)
- Let the words of my mouth, and the meditation of my heart, be acceptable in thy sight, O LORD, my strength, and my redeemer. (Psalm 19:14)
- So we thy people and the sheep of thy pasture will give thee thanks forever: we will shew forth thy praise to all generations. (Psalm 79:13)

WHAT OTHERS SAY
God gave the psalms to us so that we would give the psalms back to God. No other book of the Bible was inspired for that expressed purpose. *Donald S. Whitney*

SO WHAT?
The book of Psalms is a prayer book to help guide us in our praying.

LEARN TO PRAY. . .with Good Posture

IN TEN WORDS OR LESS
Our posture in prayer can express our heart attitude.

DETAILS, PLEASE
The Bible records no commands or exhortations about a "proper" prayer posture. Since we are told to "pray without ceasing" (1 Thessalonians 5:17), this would certainly require different positions! This is an external issue that has no bearing on our prayers being answered—what is essential are the *internal* heart issues that do affect our prayers. It might be better to ask, *What's the posture of my heart? What message is my body language expressing about my soul when I pray?*

The external and internal matters of prayer are combined in 1 Timothy 2:8, where the apostle Paul says he hopes "that men pray every where, lifting up holy hands, without wrath and doubting." These "holy hands" symbolize holy living, which does affect our prayers (Psalm 24:3–4). If people are going to raise their hands in worship and prayer, they must be "holy hands" that are free from wickedness. The phrase "without wrath" demands that we remove angry conflicts with others, which also hinders prayers (Mark 11:25–26). And the reference to "doubting" involves questioning God and His dealings with people. Our own sin problems should be our first matter of prayer—this is confession.

The Bible does describe various bodily positions used in prayer:

1. Standing acknowledged acceptance (1 Samuel 1:26)
2. Kneeling expressed humility (Daniel 6:10)
3. Being prostrate expressed total surrender (Nehemiah 8:6)
4. Bowed heads represented respect and reverence (2 Chronicles 29:30)
5. Lifting eyes heavenward recognized God's exalted position (John 17:1)
6. Lifting hands acknowledged God as the source of blessings (Psalm 63:4)
7. Facing Jerusalem acknowledged God's earthly manifestation (Daniel 6:10)
8. Lying in bed at night was useful for contemplation (Psalm 63:6)

9. Sitting before the Lord also expressed contemplation
    (2 Samuel 7:18)

A particular prayer custom may be better than having none, but that's only a matter of preference. Our contemporary style of closing our eyes and folding our hands have *no* biblical examples. The important thing is just that we pray.

ADDITIONAL SCRIPTURES

- I fell upon my knees, and spread out my hands unto the LORD my God, and said, O my God, I am ashamed and blush to lift up my face to thee. (Ezra 9:5–6)
- O come, let us worship and bow down: let us kneel before the LORD our maker. (Psalm 95:6)
- And they sang praises with gladness, and they bowed their heads and worshipped. (2 Chronicles 29:30)
- And Jesus lifted up his eyes, and said, Father, I thank thee that thou hast heard me. (John 11:41)
- And he went a little father, and fell on his face, and prayed, saying, O my Father, if it be possible, let this cup pass from me: nevertheless not as I will, but as thou wilt. (Matthew 26:39)

WHAT OTHERS SAY

Rather than external positioning, the Bible emphasizes the posture of the heart. . .the important thing is that your heart is bowed in submission to the lordship of Christ. *John MacArthur*

SO WHAT?

Since scripture recommends no one prayer posture, we can use any bodily position that helps us pray.

LEARN TO PRAY...
with Christ's Intercession

IN TEN WORDS OR LESS
Jesus, our High Priest, prays to the Father for us.

DETAILS, PLEASE
Hebrews 7:25 says that Christ "is able also to save them to the uttermost that come unto God by him, seeing he ever liveth to make intercession for them." Why is He able to save? Because of the efficacy of His sacrificial death and His prayers for His people. Jesus saves them "to the uttermost" (KJV). . ."completely" (NIV). . ."forever" (NASB). Christians can have confidence that God accepts them because of Jesus Christ's neverending prayers on their behalf as their Advocate (1 John 1:7, 9, 2:1–2).

ADDITIONAL SCRIPTURES
- Who is he that condemeth? It is Christ that died, yea rather, that is risen again, who is even at the right hand of God, who also maketh intercession for us. (Romans 8:34)
- Wherefore in all things it behoved him to be made like unto his brethren, that he might be a merciful and faithful high priest in things pertaining to God, to make reconciliation for the sins of the people. (Hebrews 2:17)
- "But I have prayed for you, Simon, that your faith may not fail. And when you are turned back, strengthen your brothers." (Luke 22:32 NIV)
- For Christ is not entered into the holy places made with hands, which are figures of the true; but into heaven itself, now to appear in the presence of God for us. (Hebrews 9:24)

WHAT OTHERS SAY
The intercessory work of Christ is invaluable to every Christian, for it makes clear that our ongoing acceptance before God is finally grounded in the utter sufficiency of the cross. *Donald A. Carson*

SO WHAT?
Because Jesus' intercession for His people is always answered, Christians can have assurance of their acceptance by God.

LEARN TO PRAY. . .
with the Spirit's Intercession

IN TEN WORDS OR LESS
God's Spirit helps when we don't know what to pray.

DETAILS, PLEASE
Romans 8 states that the Holy Spirit helps believers with their weakness in praying (verses 26–27). One issue is that "we know not what we should pray for as we ought." Our needs may be clear, but what to pray for is not always. So God provides the Spirit's intercession for help and encouragement. It is described as "groanings which cannot be uttered"—a silent work in us between God the Father and His Spirit, making our prayers effective.

ADDITIONAL SCRIPTURES
- The Father. . .shall give you another Comforter, that he may abide with you forever; even the Spirit of truth. (John 14:16–17)
- For as many as are led by the Spirit of God, they are the sons of God. For ye have not received the spirit of bondage again to fear; but ye have received the Spirit of adoption, whereby we cry, Abba, Father. (Romans 8:14–15)
- Nothing in all creation is hidden from God's sight. Everything is uncovered and laid bare before the eyes of him to whom we must give an account. (Hebrews 4:13 NIV)
- For who knows a person's thoughts except their own spirit within them? In the same way no one knows the thoughts of God except the Spirit of God. (1 Corinthians 2:11 NIV)

WHAT OTHERS SAY
The Holy Spirit lays hold of our weaknesses along with us and carries His part of the burden facing us as if two men were carrying a log, one at each end. *Archibald T. Robertson*

SO WHAT?
God provides help with our prayers. We might pray for good things, but God's Spirit knows the best things.

LEARN TO PRAY. . .without Disobedience

IN TEN WORDS OR LESS
Unconfessed sin will hinder God from answering our prayers.

DETAILS, PLEASE
Psalm 66:18 describes what keeps God from answering prayers: "If I had cherished iniquity in my heart, the Lord would not have listened" (ESV). The idea of "cherishing sin" is to have a favorable opinion of it, to think it has no consequences. The problem of unconfessed sin is intentionally positioned between the psalmist's praise to God (verses 16–17) and his report of God answering prayers (verses 19–20). Because the psalm writer honored God and dealt with his sin, he could testify that God answered his prayers.

ADDITIONAL SCRIPTURES
- The LORD is far from the wicked: but he heareth the prayer of the righteous (Proverbs 15:29)
- But your iniquities have separated between you and your God, and your sins have hid his face from you, that he will not hear. (Isaiah 59:2)
- "When you spread out your hands in prayer, I hide my eyes from you; even when you offer many prayers, I am not listening. Your hands are full of blood!" (Isaiah 1:15 NIV)
- They are turned back to the iniquities of their forefathers, which refused to hear my words; and they went after other gods to serve them: the house of Israel and the house of Judah have broken my covenant which I made with their fathers. Therefore thus saith the LORD, Behold, I will bring evil upon them, which they shall not be able to escape; and though they shall cry unto me, I will not hearken unto them. (Jeremiah 11:10–11)

WHAT OTHERS SAY
Before we conclude that God has simply not heard our prayers or that it is not His will to give us what we ask, we need to examine our hearts to see if unconfessed sin stands as a barrier between ourselves and God. *Tim Challies*

SO WHAT?
We must examine our hearts and confess any sin we discover. Then we can receive God's cleansing and blessing.

LEARN TO PRAY. . .with Abiding

In Ten Words or Less
Our prayers are answered as we abide ("remain") in Christ.

Details, Please
On the night before His death, Jesus shared a last Passover celebration with His disciples, giving them a farewell message recorded in John 13–17. This "upper room discourse" covered many important issues, including a promise of answered prayer repeated in three consecutive chapters (14:13–14; 15:7,16; 16:23–24).

In chapter 15 the Lord used an analogy to illustrate the relationship between Himself and the disciples: just as branches must remain connected to a vine to be fruitful, the disciples were to remain in fellowship with Jesus, which would glorify God (verse 8). But if they didn't "abide" in Jesus, "ye can do nothing" (verse 5).

The Lord spoke of degrees of fruitfulness: Some branches produce no fruit (verses 2, 6). These are false believers represented by Judas Iscariot (13:21–30). Other branches produce some fruit, yet others, because of the vinedresser's pruning, produce "more fruit" (verse 2). Finally, through their abiding, certain branches produce "much fruit" (verses 5, 8).

Jesus' promise in verses 7–8 shows the importance of prayer in bearing much fruit. Two conditions must be met for us to see prayers answered. Jesus said, "If ye abide in me, and my words abide in you, ye shall ask what ye will and it shall be done unto you." This *abiding* has to do with remaining and continuing. The Lord said the disciples needed to "abide in me," being united with Him by true faith that is living and active (1:12; 10:27), faithfully following Him without falling away. Secondly, Jesus' Word was to abide in them. His teaching was to be internalized, becoming part of who the disciples were. They had to believe what the Lord said and incorporate what they had learned into their lives (13:17; 17:17).

When these conditions are met, the disciples' prayers would be offered with faith, according to God's will and for His glory, and answered. Jesus' teaching was intended to reassure the disciples and give them great joy (15:11; 16:24). And His words still apply to us today.

ADDITIONAL SCRIPTURES

- And whatsoever we ask, we receive of him, because we keep his commandments, and do those things that are pleasing in his sight. (1 John 3:22)
- The LORD is near to all who call on him, to all who call on him in truth. He fulfills the desires of those who fear him; he hears their cry and saves them. (Psalm 145:18–19 NIV)
- I have written unto you young men, because ye are strong, and the word of God abideth in you, and ye have overcome the wicked one. (1 John 2:14)
- Neither have I gone back from the commandments of his lips; I have esteemed the words of his mouth more than my necessary food. (Job 23:12)

WHAT OTHERS SAY

Answered prayer is one of the first signs of a fruitful life. It is not part of the fruit itself; it is the result of a life which increasingly is becoming Christlike. The result will be, "Ask what you will." *Ray Stedman*

SO WHAT?

Since Jesus has given us promises of answered prayer, let's meet the necessary conditions—and rejoice when our prayers answered.

LEARN TO PRAY. . .
Both Audibly and Silently

IN TEN WORDS OR LESS
God hears the prayers of our mouths and our minds.

DETAILS, PLEASE
The normal biblical pattern is praying vocally rather than silently. Prayers offered in silence are acceptable, but they are the exception.

The book of Nehemiah offers an example of silent praying. Nehemiah regularly prayed for his people (1:5–11). But on one occasion, when his boss the king asked a question and awaited answer, Nehemiah "prayed to the God of heaven" (2:4) before replying. This prayer was short and silent, and God heard and answered (2:7–8).

Psalm 5 provides an example of audible praying. David referred to his words (verse 1), his cry (verse 2), and his voice (verse 3). One of the first things he did each day was ask God to hear him and lead him so that he could rejoice (verses 11–12).

ADDITIONAL SCRIPTURES
- Hannah was praying in her heart, and her lips were moving but her voice was not heard. Eli thought she was drunk. (1 Samuel 1:13 NIV)
- I cried unto the LORD with my voice; with my voice unto the LORD did I make my supplication. (Psalm 142:1)
- And at midnight Paul and Silas prayed, and sang praises unto God: and the prisoners heard them. (Acts 16:25)
- Hear my prayer, O God; give ear to the words of my mouth. (Psalm 54:2)

WHAT OTHERS SAY
Encouragingly, there is no biblical reason to believe that praying out loud is more or less effectual than praying silently. We may do either.
Bruce P. Baugus

SO WHAT?
Praying out loud or silently should not be an issue. Our concern should be spending enough time in prayer.

LEARN TO PRAY. . .for Sinning Believers

IN TEN WORDS OR LESS
Although Christians have been pardoned, intercessory prayers are still needed.

DETAILS, PLEASE
God promises to answer intercessory prayers for erring believers: "If you see any brother or sister commit a sin that does not lead to death, you should pray and God will give them life. I refer to those whose sin does not lead to death. There is a sin that leads to death. I am not saying that you should pray about that. All wrongdoing is sin, and there is a sin that does not lead to death" (1 John 5:16–17 NIV).

The recommended intercession—"you should pray"—is for restoring a believer whose sin is publicly known. Jesus prayed for the restoration of Peter, who had denied his Lord (Luke 22:32). When we learn of another person's sin, the right reaction is to *pray first*. Intercession should flow from our affection, since loving one another characterizes believers and is commanded by God (1 John 3:10, 23; 4:21). Jesus condemned a judgmental spirit that focuses on other people's sins while ignoring our own (Matthew 7:1–5).

Notice that 1 John 5 divides sin into two categories, identified by their outcome. A sin "that does not lead to death" is mentioned three times; another sin, "that leads to death," is referenced once. Though uncommon descriptions in the Bible, they are supported by other passages.

Many understand the "sin that leads to death" as referring to premature physical death as God's judgment for sin. Some biblical people were judged by God with a sudden death penalty as an act of divine justice (Acts 5:1–11; 1 Corinthians 5:5; 11:30). But the responsibility for distinguishing these two categories of sin falls to God, not to us. It's God's business to do the sorting—it's our business is to do the praying!

Sin in a person's life is always a serious issue—its why Jesus died (Romans 6:23; Hebrews 9:28; Isaiah 53:5, 12). Practically speaking, we should continue praying for anyone who is practicing sin.

ADDITIONAL SCRIPTURES
- And the prayer of faith will save the sick, and the Lord

will raise him up. And if he has committed sins, he will be forgiven. (James 5:15 NKJV)

- My servant Job shall pray for you: for him I will accept: lest I deal with you after your folly, in that ye have not spoken of me the thing which is right, like my servant Job. (Job 42:8)
- So he said he would destroy them—had not Moses, his chosen one, stood in the breach before him to keep his wrath from destroying them. (Psalm 106:23 NIV)
- Pardon, I beseech thee, the iniquity of this people according unto the greatness of thy mercy, and as thou hast forgiven this people, from Egypt even until now. (Numbers 14:19)

WHAT OTHERS SAY

The Christian. . .will recognize his duty in love to care for his brother in need whether the need which he sees be material or, as here, spiritual. He cannot say, "Am I my brother's keeper?" and do nothing. *John R. W. Stott*

SO WHAT?

Christians must confess their own sins, but we can also help others by praying "Father, forgive them."

LEARN TO PRAY. . .for Personal Peace

IN TEN WORDS OR LESS
God gives His peace to those who pray with faith.

DETAILS, PLEASE
Philippians 4 begins with an exhortation to "stand fast in the Lord." The rest of this section (verses 2–9) explains how this is done. The apostle Paul concludes by saying that if believers apply what they've learned and follow his example, "the God of peace will be with you" (verse 9). Prayer is a vital part of this process (verses 6–7).

Readers are first told not to worry: "Do not be anxious about anything" (verse 6 NIV). Anxiety ruins peace and is often brought on by prayerlessness. We can choose to worry or decide to trust God and pray. In His sermon on the mount, Jesus taught the same thing. "I tell you," He said, "do not worry about your life" (Matthew 6:25 NIV). When people worry about the problems of tomorrow—which may never actually happen—they ruin the possibility for peace today (Matthew 6:34). Jesus gently chided Martha, one of the women who followed Him, telling her, "you are worried and upset about many things" (Luke 10:41 NIV). To have peace, worrying must stop.

Next, the Philippians are told to pray. "But in everything by prayer and supplication with thanksgiving let your requests be made known unto God" (Philippians 4:6). Don't worry—be prayerful! We can be sure that God is as concerned as we are about our requests. The apostle Peter urged believers to cast "all your care upon him, for he careth for you" (1 Peter 5:7). Knowing that God cares and acts, it's important then to be thankful for the prayers He's already answered. That's why Paul mentioned supplications "with thanksgiving."

The benefit promised is an inner spiritual calm. When worrying ends and praying begins, "the peace of God, which passeth all understanding, shall keep your hearts and minds through Christ Jesus" (Philippians 4:7). This peace is not the result of some merely human technique—it is God's blessing, described in Galatians 5:22 as "the fruit of the Spirit." It is the peace predicted by the prophet Isaiah—peace "like a river," constantly flowing (Isaiah 66:12).

ADDITIONAL SCRIPTURES

- Pursue righteousness, faith, love and peace, along with those who call on the Lord out of a pure heart. (2 Timothy 2:22 NIV)
- Now the Lord of peace himself give you peace always by all means. (2 Thessalonians 3:16)
- The LORD lift up his countenance upon thee, and give thee peace. (Numbers 6:26)
- Peace I leave with you, my peace I give unto you: not as the world giveth, give I unto you. Let not your heart be troubled, neither let it be afraid. (John 14:27)
- Thou wilt keep him in perfect peace, whose mind is stayed on thee: because he trusteth in thee. (Isaiah 26:3)

WHAT OTHERS SAY

He who prays with a perfect trust in the love, wisdom, and power of God will find God's peace. The result of believing prayer is that the peace of God will stand like a sentinel on guard upon our hearts. *William Barclay*

SO WHAT?

Christians have *peace with God* through faith in Christ and experience the *peace of God* by praying about everything, worrying about nothing, and being thankful for what God has done.

LEARN TO PRAY. . .for Abounding Love

Christian are to pray for growth in true, biblical love.

DETAILS, PLEASE
Paul began his letter to the Philippians telling them they were in his prayers (1:3–4). He also told them, "I have you in my heart" (verse 7). Paul's prayers were motivated by Christ's love. Where there is love there will be prayers. We pray for those we love.

Paul's main request to God was that the Philippians themselves would have a growing love: "And this I pray, that your love may abound yet more and more." He prayed that their love would grow in both knowledge and judgment (verse 9).

Regarding knowledge, Paul wanted the church to have an intelligent love. Learning 1 Corinthians 13, known as the Bible's "love chapter," is helpful, since it is the best definition of true love. And when we study the life of Jesus in the four Gospels, we see how love is applied to life.

Regarding judgment, the Philippians' love was to be discerning. This is the ability to make distinctions between good and evil in love. This church was part of an evil society that had its own ideas about love, very much like we face today. Ephesians 5:1–7 explains the differences between the world's sinful ideas about love and real, biblical love.

Why is this growing love so important? Paul said "that ye may be sincere" (genuine and without hypocrisy), and able to make good decisions that would not be unnecessarily offensive to people. The Philippians were to keep growing as they looked to the future, influenced by an awareness of Christ's imminent return and their accountability to Him (verse 10).

Paul ends this section by saying that the Philippians' lives were to be filled with a moral beauty of righteous actions, empowered by Christ and ultimately for the glory of God (verse 11). This is how letter ends too—with a reminder that God is to be glorified (4:20).

When prayers about growing love are answered, God *is* glorified.

ADDITIONAL SCRIPTURES

- And the Lord make you to increase and abound in love one toward another, and toward all men, even as we do toward you. (1 Thessalonians 3:12)
- Seeing that ye have purified your souls in obeying the truth through the Spirit unto unfeigned love of the brethren, see that ye love one another with a pure heart fervently. (1 Peter 1:22)
- Walk in love, as Christ also hath loved us, and hath given himself for us an offering and a sacrifice to God for a sweetsmelling savour. (Ephesians 5:2)
- Beloved, if God so loved us, we ought also to love one another. (1 John 4:11)
- Owe no man anything, but to love one another: for he that loveth another hath fulfilled the law. (Romans 13:8)

WHAT OTHERS SAY

Paul often let his friends know what it was he begged of God for them, that they might know what to beg for themselves and be directed in their own prayers. . . . He prayed that they might be a loving people. *Matthew Henry*

SO WHAT?

When we are born again into God's family, He transforms our lives to make us more like Himself. Our prayers to grow in love are part of that process.

LEARN TO PRAY. . .for God's Wisdom

IN TEN WORDS OR LESS
For true knowledge and understanding, ask God—He will provide.

DETAILS, PLEASE
We all have times when we don't know how to deal with particular problems. The Bible's book of James has a simple solution: "If any of you lack wisdom let him ask of God" (1:5). Only He can give what we cannot find anywhere else: "For the LORD giveth wisdom: out of his mouth cometh knowledge and understanding" (Proverbs 2:6). This wisdom is available in God's Word and requires His illumination—so prayers for understanding are advisable: "Open my eyes that I may see wonderful things in your law" (Psalm 119:18 NIV).

To encourage us to pray, God describes Himself in James 1:5 as very generous with His wisdom—and He "upbraideth not," which means He doesn't fault us for needing wisdom. Because He is loving and patient, He is always ready to assist those who request His help.

ADDITIONAL SCRIPTURES
- Behold, the fear of the LORD, that is wisdom; and to depart from evil is understanding. (Job 28:28)
- Daniel answered and said, Blessed be the name of God for ever and ever: for wisdom and might are his. (Daniel 2:20)
- But unto them which are called, both Jews and Greeks, Christ is the power of God, and the wisdom of God. (1 Corinthians 1:24)

WHAT OTHERS SAY
The believer needs "wisdom" to see his trials in a true light and to profit spiritually from them. . .the trials that often overwhelm the godly create struggles and require God-given wisdom to resolve them. *D. Edmond Hiebert*

SO WHAT?
If you need direction, you can call on God who encourages us to pray to Him for help.

LEARN TO PRAY. . .for Restoration

IN TEN WORDS OR LESS
After God gives forgiveness, we pray for continual restoration.

DETAILS, PLEASE
Psalm 51 is a "penitential" psalm. David wrote the words in sorrow, after the prophet Nathan revealed sins the king had previously committed and covered up. Psalm 51 is written so that we too can pray its verses back to God when we need His forgiveness and restoration: "Create in me a pure heart, O God, and renew a steadfast spirit within me. Do not cast me from your presence or take your Holy Spirit from me. Restore to me the joy of your salvation and grant me a willing spirit, to sustain me" (verses 10–12 NIV).

ADDITIONAL SCRIPTURES
- After Job had prayed for his friends, the LORD restored his fortunes and doubled his previous possessions. (Job 42:10 CSB)
- "But I have prayed for you, Simon, that your faith may not fail. And when you have turned back, strengthen your brothers." (Luke 22:32 NIV)
- Remember therefore from whence thou art fallen, and repent, and do the first works; or else I will come unto thee quickly, and remove thy candlestick out of his place, except thou repent. (Revelation 2:5)

WHAT OTHERS SAY
[In Psalm 51] David pleads for more than forgiveness. He pleads for renewal. He is passionately committed to being changed by God.
John Piper

SO WHAT?
Forgiveness is just the beginning of the road back from where we have fallen. The road of restoration is uphill, but well worth the climb.

LEARN TO PRAY. . .for Enemies

IN TEN WORDS OR LESS
Praying for those who hate us is imitating Jesus.

DETAILS, PLEASE
In Luke 6 Jesus told His followers, "Love your enemies, do good to them which hate you, bless them that curse you, and pray for them which despitefully use you" (verses 27–28). This high standard of love for enemies is an unnatural response to mistreatment—it is the fruit of God's Spirit (Galatians 5:22). Praying for enemies also produces benefits such as a great reward from God (verse 23) and confirmation that we are "children of the Highest" (verse 35).

ADDITIONAL SCRIPTURES
- Then said Jesus, Father, forgive them; for they know not what they do. (Luke 23:34)
- Rejoice not when thine enemy falleth, and let not thine heart be glad when he stumbleth. (Proverbs 24:17)
- Therefore if thine enemy hunger, feed him; if he thirst, give him drink: for in so doing thou shalt heap coals of fire on his head. (Romans 12:20)
- Do not repay evil with evil or insult with insult. On the contrary, repay evil with blessing, because to this you were called so that you may inherit a blessing. (1 Peter 3:9 NIV)
- When a man's ways please the LORD, he maketh even his enemies to be at peace with him. (Proverbs 16:7)

WHAT OTHERS SAY
Prayer for your enemies is one of the deepest forms of love, because it means that you have to really want that something good happen to them. *John Piper*

SO WHAT?
Remember that before God saved us, He was patient with us as *His* enemies. We should pray that He will be patient with *our* enemies—and save them.

LEARN TO PRAY. . .
and Understand Imprecatory Prayers

IN TEN WORDS OR LESS
Imprecatory prayers request God's righteous judgment on His enemies.

DETAILS, PLEASE
Imprecations are prayers asking God to judge His enemies. These prayers are perplexing since they seem to contradict Jesus' teaching about loving our enemies.

Imprecatory prayers are found in the psalms. An example is Psalm 69:24: "Pour out thine indignation upon them, and let thy wrathful anger take hold of them." These words were written by King David, Israel's leader, who was viewed as God's appointed representative on earth governing God's chosen nation. So opposing David was considered opposing God. Keeping imprecatory prayers in their historical context helps to understand them.

These prayers do not condone personal vengeance, since that is not permitted in either the Old Testament (Leviticus 19:17–18; Deuteronomy 32:35) or the New (Romans 12:19–20). When the anointed-but-not-yet-crowned David fled from the jealous King Saul, he repeatedly resisted opportunities to be vengeful (1 Samuel 24, 26).

Christians are never permitted to be vindictive. It is the prerogative of God alone to repay His opponents. He commands our patience with enemies because that is how He treats His own adversaries, giving them time for repentance.

It's best to understand Old Testament imprecations in the light of New Testament warnings. Consider Jesus' two-sided gospel message in John 3. There's a promise of eternal life for believers (verses 16–17) and warnings of judgment for those who reject Him (verses 18, 36). Since God has warned of the serious outcome of rejecting Him, the imprecations can be viewed as simply asking God to do what He already said He would do. Jesus Himself spoke pronouncements against false prophets (Matthew 7:15–23), unrepentant Galilean cities (Matthew 11:20–24), and hypocritical scribes and Pharisees (Matthew 23:13–33). Also note the apostle Paul's warning in 1 Corinthians 16:22 and the scene of martyred souls, praying for justice, in Revelation 6:9–10.

Imprecations have an evangelistic purpose. The psalm writer Asaph said, "Fill their faces with shame; that they may seek thy name, O LORD" (Psalm 83:16). Asaph asked God to bring whatever hardship was needed into people's lives so that they will seek His salvation. Pastor and author John Piper has said it well: "Prayers of imprecation should not be our first reaction to evil, but our last."

ADDITIONAL SCRIPTURES

- Bless them which persecute you: bless, and curse not. (Romans 12:14)
- But I say unto you, love your enemies, bless them that curse you, do good to them that hate you, and pray for them that despitefully use you, and persecute you. (Matthew 5:44)
- Do not take revenge, my dear friends, but leave room for God's wrath, for it is written: "It is mine to avenge; I will repay," says the Lord. (Romans 12:19 NIV)

WHAT OTHERS SAY

We lift our voices, not our swords, as we pray for God to either convert or curse the enemies of Christ and His kingdom. *John W. Tweeddale*

SO WHAT?

Christians should speak the truth in love, perform acts of kindness, and ask God to be faithful to His promises and warnings.

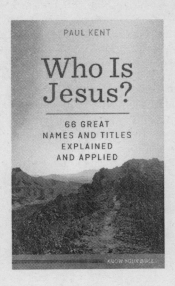